The Way To Live 1.0.1

Joshua Keith Craft // @joshuakcraft

ISBN: 978-1-7330945-9-7 (Paperback), 979-8-9874069-0-8(e-book)

1% Publishing
8500 Teel Parkway
Frisco, TX 75034
(214)387-9833

ABOUT THE AUTHOR

Joshua Craft's personal mission statement is to learn to live in a way that shows others the way to live. He is the son of Keith Craft, Lead Pastor at Elevate Life in Frisco, Texas. He considers it one of his greatest honors to carry on his father's legacy personally and professionally. He Co-Pastors Elevate Life, serves as his dad's self-proclaimed consigliere, and coaches entrepreneurs and business leaders in practical philosophy, Joshua also helps to lead Man Academy, Upgrade Your Human and Freedom coaching networks alongside Steve Weatherford. He has been married to his wife Courtnei for 8 years and they have two daughters, Charlie Monroe and Harper Elizabeth.

WHY 1.0.1?

It's taken me my entire lifetime - 35 years - to develop the philosophy in this book. In March of 2020 when the world shut down, I took time to write out my personal philosophy of life to pass down to my children someday. My dad convinced me to turn it into a book. This book represents the best current version of this personal philosophy of life. I don't think this book will ever be fully finished. Just like my philosophy won't be fully finished. Just like you, I am always learning and growing in an attempt to become the person God has created me to be. I anticipate that I will update this book as frequently as I update my own personal philosophy. I hope that this book helps you to learn how to live the life God created you to live, so that you can show the people God has put in your life how to do the same thing.

- Josh

CONTENTS //

THE PAST IS PROLOGUE

"The time will come when diligent research over long periods will bring to light things which now lie hidden. A single lifetime, even though entirely devoted to the sky, would not be enough for the investigation of so vast a subject... And so this knowledge will be unfolded only through long successive ages. There will come a time when our descendants will be amazed that we did not know things that are so plain to them... Many discoveries are reserved for ages still to come, when memory of us will have been effaced." [1]

// Seneca

Everything written here is only here because of what came before. Without those before us, we would have nothing to contribute.

Our role is to connect the dots for current generations, just as those who came before us. What we teach will always remain unfinished. Never complete. It is up to those who come after us to connect their own dots and make the world a better place for their generation.

Every generation passes things down. Most generations will only pass down temporal knowledge: knowledge of the things that change. The striving for riches, the vanity of fame, the fleeting nature of influence.

Some generations pass down something greater: eternal knowledge. Knowledge about the things that do not change. Virtue. Wisdom. Purpose. Meaning. Things that have been here before us and will long outlive us. It has become too rare for those who come before us to lead us into wisdom.

Too many generations have had to start over because the generation that came before them did not pass down true wisdom. Let us, in this generation, not find ourselves guilty of doing the same.

Because of those that came before me, I do not find myself starting over. I find myself building on a foundation laid for me by those who have paid a tremendous cost. Not just me but all of us. How many wise people have walked the earth and blazed a trail for us to follow? These people have laid a foundation for us. A foundation of eternal wisdom.

Each one of us also have people in our lives that show us the way. Keith Craft is my father of origin. He is also my father of choice. He is not the wisest man to ever live. But he is the wisest man I've ever known. He is my hero. He embodies what I strive to be as a man, father, husband and leader.

The virtues that shape my thinking, lead my attitudes and guide my behavior are not things I discovered on my own. I was (and still am) taught by him, who I consider to be a true master.

It can be trite, but it's true: words cannot express the impact of my dad on my life, and therefore, the impact he will have on any life God gives me the privilege to influence.

What is written here, and my life itself, is only what it is because of the price paid to build a foundation for me to stand on. All that I am or hope to be I owe to my father.

My hope is that as you read this, you discover the power of your own life. Like many people, you may be starting over. That's hard, but I promise you it's worth it. Because my dad started over, I don't have to. This book is dedicated to his life and influence.

0 // HOW TO EAT AN ELEPHANT

"What's the best way to eat an elephant? One bite at a time."

Most of us have heard this phrase. It's commonly attributed to **Bishop Desmond Tutu**, a South African anti-apartheid and human rights activist.

This phrase resonates with us because life feels big. Living life often feels like trying to eat an elephant. We make progress, the days are long, but the years are short. Although progress of every form has marked human history since its beginning, one question continues to gnaw at us no matter what era we were born into, our culture, our status, or any other way we try to define ourselves.

That question is - **"What is the way to live a good life?"**

You may phrase this question differently, but your question is most likely similar to mine. Where can we discover purpose, meaning and destiny? Is there such a thing? Is life meant to have meaning or are we just a heap of atoms who happen to exist at this present moment for no particular purpose? Figuring this out is like trying to eat an elephant.

Before we can look into this question and think through our answers, it's important to consider what it takes to eat an elephant.

Elephants are the largest animals on the earth. They stand up to eleven feet tall and can weigh almost eight tons (16,000 lb.). Their skin can also be up to one inch thick in certain places.

Considering this, how long would it take you or I to kill an elephant? How long would it take for us to prepare an elephant to be eaten? Then, how long would it take us to actually eat it? There's a lot that goes into the process of eating an elephant.

This is a helpful metaphor for what we are attempting to do with the big questions of life—specifically the question of how to live and what creates meaning for us.

I have good news. We don't have to create a plan for how we eat an elephant. We just have to follow the one already made. Believe it or not, the plan itself is pretty obvious. Simple even. But simple ≠ easy.

As we know, throughout human history we have attempted to answer these big questions. Those who have come before us have made their attempts. We are making our attempts now. And in the future, those who come after us will try. So is human history. We are born to pursue eternal knowledge.

I think God knew this from the jump. I think he actually designed us this way. Why does this matter? Because in storytelling, the way a story is told matters just as much as the content of the story itself. God has been telling a story since the beginning of history. The story of history. The structure of this story is important because it helps us to clearly see the plan for how we eat the elephant..

The Apostle Paul says it this way in Romans 1:

"For ever since the world was created, people have seen the earth

and sky. Through everything God made, they can clearly see his invisible qualities—his eternal power and divine nature. So they have no excuse for not knowing God."

// Romans 1:20

Since the beginning of time, God has made himself clear. His qualities, nature and even his plan have played out over the entirety of human history. This plan provides a template for how we should live our lives today. This plan has been given to us in generation-sized chunks as we made progress and understood more. As Seneca told us, the things that seem ground-breaking and revelational to us now will be commonplace to those that come after us. And we cannot hope to fathom the discoveries that our descendants will uncover.

There is a design, a plan that underpins the human story. We are on a road to somewhere. We may not know where, but the author of the plan does. Looking at the past, we can see the path previous generations have trod, the foundation they—and God—laid for us to build upon.

Simply, the plan looks like this.

Part one //
> *Know God.*
> We must understand God has a plan for humanity as a whole and us individually.

Part two //
> *Know yourself.*
> We must do what those before us have done for thousands of years: seek wisdom and understand what gives us meaning and purpose.

Part three //

>*Decide your role.*
>We must determine what the impact of our life should be
>to the world around us.

This is just an introduction, so I'm not going to throw the elephant
in front of you now and ask you to figure it out. But that's the journey we will be taking. This is not a textbook, nor is it meant to be.
What I write is my perspective, paraphrase, and understanding. Ultimately, you should determine for yourself the way you want to live,
and this book is meant to help you on that journey. Building your
philosophy of life requires work on your part. There is an appendix
of works I have been inspired by at the end of this book. Use this
for supplemental reading if you want to look further into some of
the topics I discuss in this book.

Finally, these thoughts—just like any philosophy—are always changing and will always require updates and revisions. It will never be
finished because there is always a better way. A better way to think,
a better way to act, and a better way to live.

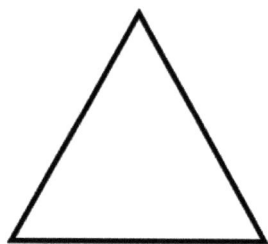

0.5 // CONNECT THE DOTS

•••

We all have dots. Experiences, events, moments, and memories. We go through life, and meaningful things happen to us. These things are points in time, or dots, that we go back to.

The thing about dots is that they end up connecting to each other.

///

We all have lines. Lines are what give the dots meaning. We use lines to connect our dots. We do this by saying, "Here's what this meant to me" or "Here's what I learned." Sometimes we connect dots by saying, "I'll never go to that place again" or "I'm glad that's over." We connect dots in our life to make sense of ourselves and the world around us. We decide which direction the lines point, but all of us have lines that connect our dots together.

The thing about lines is that they turn into shapes.

△

The moments (dots) become meaning (lines). The meaning we give to moments creates the shape of our life. The shape of our lives is dictated by how we choose to connect our dots. The meaning that we give our moments is what makes us who we are.

There is something about groups of three:

- ▲ Faith, hope, and love.
- ▲ Stop, look, and listen.
- ▲ Good stories have a beginning, middle, and end.
- ▲ In photography there is the rule of thirds.
- ▲ The trinity is Father, Spirit, and Son.
- ▲ We all have a past, present, and future.
- ▲ We are spirit, soul, and body.
- ▲ There are three blind mice,
- ▲ Three little pigs,
- ▲ Three musketeers,
- ▲ Three stooges and three wise men.
- ▲ In the United States, the Declaration of Independence states our unalienable rights are life, liberty, and the pursuit of happiness.
- ▲ We want a government of the people, by the people, and for the people.
- ▲ We give our blood, sweat, and tears to the causes we support.
- ▲ We tell our friends, Romans, and countrymen that we came, we saw, and we conquered.
- ▲ Schoolhouse Rock even taught us that three is a magic number.

A triangle has three points connected by three lines. A point by itself is not a triangle, neither is a line. This is simple for us to understand. Lines and points are not triangles. But if they are arranged in a certain way, they can form a triangle.

There are three dots we must connect in life //

Knowing God
Knowing ourselves
Deciding our role

Those are the most significant dots we can ever connect. Connecting those dots will allow you to see your life as a triangle. There are things inside and outside of that triangle. But we'll get to that. Let's start with the first dot.

DOT I // GOD

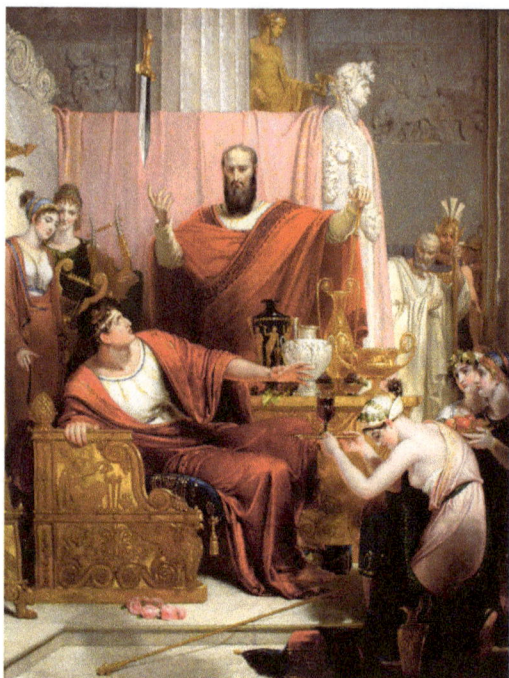

1 // THE QUESTION

"An unexamined life is not worth living." // **Socrates**

The philosopher Cicero tells a story of Dionysus II, the king of Syracuse in the fourth and fifth centuries BC. He was rich and powerful, but remarkably unhappy. He ruled with an iron fist and made many enemies as king.

He lived under the constant fear of assassination. In fact, it is believed that his bedchamber was surrounded by a moat on all sides to prevent would-be assassins from killing him in his sleep.

In Cicero's story, a man named Damocles lavished Dionysus with compliments and stated how full of joy his life must be.

"Since this life delights you," Dionysus said to Damocles, "do you wish to taste it yourself and make a trial of my good fortune?"

When Damocles agreed, Dionysus seated him on a large golden couch and ordered his servants to wait on Damocles hand and foot. He was treated to the best food and drink that Syracuse had to offer. Damocles couldn't believe it. He was getting to live the life of a king.

As soon as he had begun to fully enjoy his experience, he looked toward the ceiling. The happiness he felt left him as quickly as it had come. Hanging from the ceiling, just above his head was a sword. Suspended only by a single strand of horsehair.

From that moment on, Damocles could no longer enjoy the couch, the food, the drinks or the servants. After casting several glances at the sword dangling above him by a thread, he asked to be excused saying that he no longer wished to be as fortunate as Dionysus.

How many of us look at those we see as successful and wonder what good fortune they must have while we experience the worst of it? How many people have we seen find "happiness" only to see their lives get worse because of it? How many times do we look at those who have more money, success or influence and wish to sit where they sit, not taking time to glance at the precariousness of their—as well as our—own sword of Damocles?

Maybe we are all like Dionysus in some way. Blessed abundantly, but we have eyes that only see the instability of our fortune. Maybe we are like Damocles and wish to sit in the seat of others, not understanding the precariousness of their experience as well.

Take a minute and ask yourself this question - **What do you want out of life?**

A good job? Nice house? Caring spouse? Money? Success? Influence? Happiness?

These are just some of the things that all of us want out of life. Sometimes we look at things like this and really do believe that attaining these things will eventually help us to accomplish some grand purpose.

We can know minute by minute what we want. Or even decade by decade. But what do you want out of your whole life? Out of all the things you could seek out and pursue, what do you think is most valuable?

The sword of Damocles teaches us that happiness can be lost at any time. Much of what we spend our lives doing can, in a moment, become meaningless.

Have you ever taken the time to decide what you want out of life? What would be worth your effort, strife and toil in your short time on Earth?

Have you considered that for all your striving and effort you could actually mis-live? That you could miss the point of your entire existence and live a life that is unfulfilling and meaningless? Culture offers us many things that seem valuable. How many times have we heard of people regretting their pursuit of society's definition of happiness? How many times have we pursued fame, fortune, influence and power hoping they would make us feel less empty?

For centuries, people have searched the world over for gold. For centuries, untrained prospectors have also been fooled by pyrite, now known as fool's gold. Pyrite looks like gold and is often found next to gold deposits, but it isn't gold. Even though they can look similar if we're not paying attention, gold and pyrite couldn't be more different. Today (2022) gold can sell for up to $2,000 an ounce while pyrite sells for $0.16 an ounce.

Living a life without deciding what we want out of it is a lot like an untrained prospector finding pyrite. Once we find something that seems valuable, we can feel as though we've struck it rich, but we are despondent when we discover the truth.

Just like it is possible to live a good life, it is also possible to live a bad life. This is not something we often want to think about, but we should think about it now. The fact that we can think about it today means we can determine not to mis-live—not to live a bad life—starting now. It's that simple. But **simple ≠ easy**.

As Maria says in *The Sound of Music*, "Let's start at the very beginning, that's a very good place to start."

Start right now, decide what you want out of life.

What do you want out of life? That's a big question.

To determine what you want out of life, you should decide how you will measure your life. At the end of your life, what will you measure to determine whether you were successful?

Not sure? What do most people on their deathbed wish for, long for or find joy in? Their money? Their status? At the end of their life, most people measure the success of their life according to the quality of their relationships. The regrets of dying people aren't for more hours at work, more influence, a bigger house or a better job. They wish for more and better relationships. They wish to have made a bigger impact on the lives of the people around them.[2]

A former hospice nurse, **Bonnie Ware**, wrote a book titled *Top Five Regrets of the Dying* filled with her career-long observations of dying people. The top five wishes she identified were:

1. The wish for the courage to live a life true to themselves, not the life others expected of them.
2. The wish that they hadn't worked so hard. Every male patient she encountered felt they missed their children's youth and partner's companionship.

3. The wish that they would have had the
   courage to express their feelings.
4. The wish that they had stayed in touch with their friends.
5. The wish that they had realized happiness was a choice.[3]

The *Harvard Study for Adult Development* is one of the longest studies ever done on adult life. Begun in 1938 with 268 Harvard sophomores, the study continues today with over 1,300 of these men's offspring as well as other families from around Boston. Overwhelmingly, this study provides evidence that the greatest predictor of a good life is the quality of a person's relationships. The key to mental, physical and emotional health is relationships.[4]

How many of us live our lives and prioritize our focus as if relationships are the most important thing? Not many. Think about the people in your life. I would venture to say that the happiest and healthiest people you know also have some of the best friendships, marriages and relationships. Both anecdotally and through research, we see that the greatest thing we can measure our life by is the quality of our relationships.

We know this, but do we do this? Do you or I really measure our life by the quality of our relationships? Is that our pursuit? Is that what keeps us up at night? Thinking, "How can I improve my relationships?" Most people don't embrace this way of thinking until they are dying. What if we lived with this understanding while we were still living? Understand that our lives are terminal, and at the end of our lives, we will have wished to make an impact on those closest to us.

This is universal across religion, race, creed or status. This is in the heart of every person who has or will walk the face of this earth.

Our greatest contribution to the world is the gift of our life to those people we encounter every day.

Considering all these things, here's two questions you and I should answer.

How will I measure my life?
What do I want out of life?

One day you will die. At the end of your life, what will you think of your life? What will you say to yourself?

A eulogy is a speech given at a funeral in praise of someone. Imagine the day of your funeral, your best friend gets up to deliver your eulogy. What do you want them to say about you? What do you want the people around you to feel and think about you after you are gone?

The way you answer those questions about then should determine how you will answer these questions now.

Take some time and think about those two questions. This is your life, what do you want out of it?

"To laugh often and much; to win the respect of intelligent people and the affection of children; to earn the appreciation of honest critics and endure the betrayal of false friends; to appreciate beauty; to find the beauty in others; to leave the world a bit better whether by a healthy child, a garden patch, or a redeemed social condition; to know that one life has breathed easier because you lived here. This is to have succeeded."

// **Ralph Waldo Emerson**

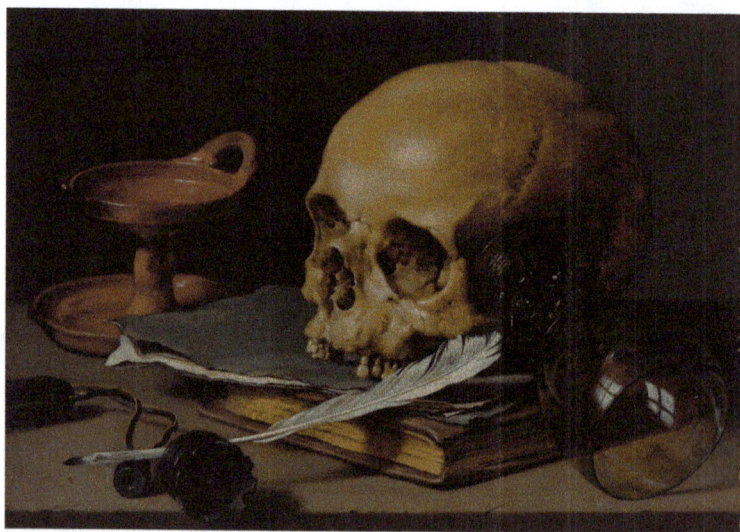

2 // THE MEANING

In answering the questions, "What do I want out of life?" and "How will I measure my life?" you may arrive at the same answers I did.

What do I want out of life? *To have a meaningful existence to me and others.*

How will I measure my life? *The impact I made in the lives of those closest to me.*

Now that I know I want my life to mean something, I must ask myself the next question:
How can my life mean something?

This may be the ultimate question. "What is the meaning of life?"

Every religion, philosophy, seminar and personality profile is committed to help us answer this question. Yet we still wrestle with meaning as much as we ever have . I would hope that after millions (or thousands, depending on your beliefs) of years of human existence, we would have made a little more progress in this regard. Even though we are taught that life has meaning, most people seem to lead meaningless lives.

Growing up in church, I heard that question asked this way, "What is your calling?" It seemed like somehow, the big answer to the purpose of my life was right in front of my face, yet I was simultaneously blind to it. When I asked how I can discover my calling, the conversation became progressively more confusing. Was it the nine spiritual gifts in 1 Corinthians 12, or the seven in Romans 12? Was it both? What about the five gifts in Ephesians 4? Or the eight more that are listed later in 1 Corinthians 12? This was troublesome for me. I have a hard enough time doing things that I understand I should do. How can I possibly hope to figure out something as vague as a calling?

Whether its wrestling with Scripture or a personality test, trying to find meaning or a calling seems unachievable. No wonder we've had such a hard time living a meaningful life.

I love simplicity. I've spent a good amount of my life trying to find a simple answer to this question of meaning. And I realized something. We are asking a question that has already been answered. In Scripture, the God that created us gave us one verse that answers the question of meaning. The apostle Paul says:

> *"Don't copy the behavior and customs of this world, but let God transform you into a new person by changing the way you think. Then you will learn to know God's will for you, which is good and pleasing and perfect."*
>
> **// Romans 12:2**

Read this portion of scripture in reverse.

God's will for your life is good and pleasing and perfect. The way to know his will for your life is to transform into a new person by changing the way that you think. The behavior and customs of this world will not teach you to do this.

This may seem basic to you, but when I read this verse this way, it

2 // THE MEANING

really did change my life. God created me as one of one. The meaning of my life is for me to be the best me that I can possibly be. How can I do this? By allowing God to change my thinking.

Most of us (Christian or not) are pursuing the same things as everyone else and are achieving the same results. Namely, lack of meaning and purpose. I don't believe this to be intentional. We all struggle with impostor syndrome. We're human. We will pretend like we know what we are doing, even when we know we don't. We do our best to keep up appearances, just like the rest of the world. We think that our meaning is found in a calling, gift, personality profile or something else. Call it a "calling," "will of God" or a "meaning of life." All of us are trying to figure out what that is for us as individuals. Yet the answer to the question of "what is it?" is so elusive.

Christians will try to convince you otherwise, but look at our reputation (especially in America) and compare that to the New Testament. You will see how many self-proclaimed Christians are well versed in the "behavior and customs" of everyone else.

What many of us notice is that the behavior and customs of Jesus are not the behavior and customs of many people who claim to be Christian. You already know this without me saying it, so let's say that the playing field is level for all of us regardless of belief system concerning the will of God and trying to understand it or live it out.

"We [need] to stop asking about the meaning of life, and instead to think of ourselves as those who were being questioned by life—daily and hourly. Our answer must consist, not in talk and meditation, but in right action and in right conduct. Life ultimately means taking the responsibility to find the right answer to its problems and to fulfill the tasks which it constantly sets for each individual...questions about the meaning of life can never be answered by sweeping

statements. 'Life' does not mean something vague, but something very real and concrete, just as life's tasks are also very real and concrete. They form man's destiny, which is different and unique for each individual. No man and no destiny can be compared with any other man or any other destiny. No situation repeats itself, and each situation calls for a different response."[5]

// Viktor Frankl

Viktor Frankl said it better than I could. Most of us will live our lives believing that we are asking the question, "What is the meaning of life?" We think that we are asking this question and that life will provide an answer for us. Maybe God will speak to us directly, or we will have a mountain-top experience with a sensei who will finally help us understand what our life means. We go through life as if we are asking the question, continually searching for the answer. We think that a relationship will answer this question. A job. A house. A car. Power, prestige, wealth and influence. We go from place to place, person to person. And we never feel like this question gets answered for us.

That is the problem. We think we are asking the question. We think that the question of "What is the meaning of life?" is meant to be answered for us by something external to us. A person, place, or thing will come along and give us meaning and purpose.

"What is the meaning of life?" is a question that we are supposed to answer. Not ask. Life—existence itself—asks this question of us, and we must have an answer. We are not supposed to be asking the question. We are supposed to be answering it through the way that we live our life every day. Romans 12:2, live your life to be the best you that only you can be. When you become your best, your life begins to mean something more than you ever thought it could.

Purpose isn't discovered, it is created.

Everything that exists, exists for a purpose. A knife has a specific purpose. If a knife didn't have a knife's purpose, it would not exist. The purpose of the knife necessitates its existence. A knife doesn't one day discover its purpose. The knife plays its role, and in playing its role, it fulfills its purpose. Now, there are clear differences between knives and humans; however, we are similar in that without purpose and meaning we wouldn't exist. Unlike kitchen utensils, we get to decide the role we play in the world. In deciding the role we play, we get to decide what our life means. Too many people go through life and wait for purpose to find them. They go through life like an inanimate object, just waiting to be used by someone or something, somewhere at some point.

Imagine you're working at an airline counter and I'm asking you a question. "How do I get from Texas to Hawaii? Instead of answering my question, you turn around and ask me, "I don't know, how do you get from Texas to Hawaii?" How confusing is that? What if you really don't know the answer? What if you didn't know cars, boats and planes existed. This journey would seem impossible.

Let's continue the analogy. You and I work for the airline. The people in our lives are our customer. To help people get to where they want to go, we have to know how to get there ourselves. We must know the way so that we can show the way.

So, the question "what is the meaning of your life?" is not a question you get to ask. It's a question you get to answer. It is a question that life asks of you. Your existence asks this question, and the life you choose to live is the answer. What does your life mean to your friends? Your family? Your spouse? Your children?

Meaning cannot be "found" or "discovered"—only created. God

created your life to mean something. The meaning of your life is created by you.

How will you measure your life?
What do you want out of life?
What is the meaning of your life?

These three questions all ask the same thing: How are you going to live?

The way I answer these questions will determine how I live.

It will affect how I see how things are "supposed" to be.

It will affect how I see everything that happens to me.

It will affect how I feel about things that happen to me.

It will affect what I decide to do about things that happen to me.

Philosophy and meaning

The word "*philosophy*" is largely confined to academic circles today. Most of the time when we think about philosophy, we think about books that are one thousand pages long that somehow say nothing and solve nothing. We think about old, poorly dressed men who ask questions that don't have an answer and identify problems that can never be solved. This is not what philosophy is supposed to be. In fact, all of us are philosophers, and we practice philosophy every day. The original meaning of the word is the pursuit and love of wisdom.

Philosophy is thinking through and deciding what is right and good and applying those things to your life with your actions. How you decide to live displays to the world what your philosophy is, how you define a good life. The way you live will be what determines if your life is meaningful. Philosophy is like the boat or plane that gets you from Texas to Hawaii. Philosophy takes us from where we are today to a better life tomorrow. A meaningful life.

What does God want us to do? To realize our potential by allowing his thinking to transform us. We shouldn't just pursue meaning. We should pursue wisdom. Wisdom is the thinking of God. Wisdom is eternal knowledge–knowledge of unchanging principles, virtues, and knowledge of what it means for your life to have meaning. Think like God thinks and watch what you think about become how you live. We owe it to the world, God, and ourselves to not just consider what our life means. We must decide that it means something and commit ourselves completely to making our lives meaningful so we can impact the lives of everyone we encounter. We must decide to become good philosophers.

Think about the three questions below as you read the rest of this book. You may not want to, or be able to, answer them right now, but at least take some time to ponder them. Remember, the way that we eat an elephant is by taking one bite at a time. In the next chapter, we will begin walking step by step through that challenge.

You have the power and responsibility to make your life mean something. Empowering yourself and taking responsibility starts with making the decision to live a meaningful life. Living a meaningful life starts with answering these questions.

How will you measure your life?
What do you want out of life?
What is the meaning of your life?

3 // THE BOOK

The beginning of our journey is the decision that our lives are meaningful. What comes with this decision must be a commitment to discover, develop and deploy that meaning.

Once we decide to do that, we are on the journey and we've taken the first bites of our elephant. Let's start with the Bible.

The Bible is believed by many to be the most influential collection of writing in human history. It is estimated that over 100 million copies are sold annually.

If you're unfamiliar with the Bible, it is not one book, it is a collection of sixty-six books.

Most scholars believe that these books were written at different times by as many as forty different authors over a 1,500-year period. That's the same amount of time from the Medieval period until now.

The oldest book in the Bible according to most scholars is either Genesis or Job, written around 1400 BC, 3,400 years ago. The newest book in the Bible is Revelation, written around 90 AD.

The Bible is divided into two parts, the Old Testament and the New Testament. There's a four-hundred-year silent period between them where nothing was written. The books of the Old Testament represent some of the first chronicles we have about human history. They are not just religiously significant, they are historically, sociologically and culturally significant, showing how people lived, what their customs and culture were, and how they interacted with each other. The Bible, regardless of our belief system, reveals much to us.

The word "*testament*" is a Latin term for "*covenant*." In the ancient world, covenants governed relationships, property disputes, and businesses. Imagine making a friend a promise and knowing that your children and their children would also keep that same promise. Covenants were like contracts that never ended. A covenant is a deep, abiding promise. Marriage is a modern-day expression of a covenant relationship.

When we look at the Bible, we are looking at many different perspectives over a long period of time that detail two things: an "old" promise and a "new" promise. And these promises are the deepest, most solemn promises that can exist.

The Bible shows us that the that the story of humanity is a structured one. The content of our story as humans is important, but so is the structure of our story. The story of humanity, from its origin to now, has much to show us. The Old Testament gives us a glimpse of the beginning of humanity. It also shows us the starting point in our own lives. When do we start to determine how to live and what makes life meaningful? When can we begin to allow God's thinking to invade our thinking? The story of humanity chronicled in Scripture shows us over thousands of years the journey that God has for us.

4 // THE PROMISE

In Genesis 12, a man named Abram is from a wealthy and successful family. This man Abram will one day become Abraham, the father of what we now call the Abrahamic religions, Judaism, Christianity and Islam.

In this story, God starts by telling Abram to leave everything he knows and go to a new place he's never been. Imagine this is you, and if you don't believe in God, pretend you do for this exercise. The omnipotent, omniscient and omnipresent God is talking directly to you about your life. God, who exists outside of time and space itself— in fact the creator of time and space itself—steps into your speck of a life at this point in history and tells you where you fit into the cosmic plan and what you need to do next.

This is something many of us wish God would do right now. "God just tell me exactly what to do about everything and I'll go do it." At least, that's what I wish.

God goes further. He makes Abram a promise, and he even changes his name from Abram to Abraham. He promises Abraham he's going to be the father of many nations. Something that we see as true today but seemed impossible at the time. Abraham is believed to be in his late seventies when God makes this promise, and he had no children.

When God changes his name, he also makes Abraham a promise. A covenant. Remember covenant? This promise is the promise. The

Old Testament, the old covenant, is this covenant that God makes to Abraham. Part one in the story that God is telling, this kicks off the whole thing.

What is so important about this covenant? I introduced the idea of covenants in Chapter 3, but think about this time in history. You were only as good as your word. A covenant was a binding contract between two parties. There were privileges, stipulations, and responsibilities for each party. Often a covenant that was made in one generation endured for generations after. If your father made a covenant with someone else's father, you were bound to honor that covenant, same with your children.

Covenants also were usually made between parties that saw each other as equals. It created an interdependency. People on both sides of the covenant were required to do their part to "uphold their end of the bargain."

Considering the covenant that God made with Abraham, it is important that we understand this. Why? Because we are not, and never will be, on equal footing with the divine. God chose to make a covenant with Abraham and his people despite this disparity.

Abraham, just like you and I, had absolutely nothing to offer God.

I know a wealthy person who was once given a Christmas present by a friend. On the outside of the box, it said, "for the man who has everything." What was inside the box? You guessed it, nothing.

That kind of gift is what Abraham brought to the covenant with

God. It was not equal. Far from it. God got nothing and Abraham got everything.

This is the first key that we must understand to live the way we're supposed to.

As the Old Testament progresses, we see that this plan—Abraham's covenant—was only for one group of people. One family. Abraham's blood relatives. God chose them and set them apart especially for him. Throughout the Old Testament, he leads them, guides them, creates laws for them and gives them a country to live in. All this promising and planning only applied to them.

Abraham had a son named Isaac; Isaac had a son named Jacob. Just as God changed the name of Abram to Abraham, he changed Jacob's name to Israel. All of Jacob's children and their descendants came to be known as the children of Israel, or Israelites. The thread of Abraham's promise continued to weave its way through his family as well.

The stories of the Old Testament are the stories of this family. Most of us today lie outside of this family. We are called Gentiles. We are outsiders to the promise God made to Abraham in the Old Testament because the promise of Abraham was only for his family. This was also true for the people who Abraham and his family lived around. The laws and regulations of the covenant they made with God weren't applicable to the Gentiles. That also meant the promises weren't either.

The journey of Abraham and his family over the span of human history represents something significant: God keeps his promises. To this day, there are descendants of Abraham walking the earth, living in the land God gave to them. The contributions of Jews to the world are countless. Despite terrible hardships, this one family—the Jewish people—has seen God fulfill his promise for generations.

Why does the Old Testament matter to Gentiles then? We understand why it matters to the family of Abraham. We also see laws in the book of Leviticus that are hard to understand in the modern world. "Don't wear makeup. Don't get tattoos or earrings or mark your body." The reason why these laws mattered to the family of Israel is because they were supposed to be special. They were asked to follow special laws that set them apart. There are Jews today that still follow many of these laws to set themselves apart. There are also people in fundamentalist Christian circles who have come to believe that we should still strive to follow these laws so that we can be "holy" and set apart.

But these laws were only meant to set the family of Abraham apart. We could follow them, but we still wouldn't be set apart. Because if you're not in the family, you're not in the family. Technically, you can still follow the rules, but it won't mean anything if you're not in the family. The rules might be good rules, but they don't get you into the family. Following the laws didn't set the Israelites apart from the Gentiles because they were already chosen by God to be set apart. Following the laws God set reminded them and everyone else in a tangible way every day that they were chosen by God.

The Old Testament for many of us is a confusing picture of God. One day he is extending mercy to a murderer. The next day he's telling people to kill women and children. How is that God loving or kind or benevolent? He seems angry and capricious.

Think about it this way. I'm a parent. I love and enjoy my children (most of the time). The problem is that I don't really enjoy other people's kids. I never have. I still don't. The things other people's kids do irritate me. I'm annoyed at watching the way other people's children behave. I don't mind when my child cries and screams on an airplane, but when I see a person get on a plane with a baby, my first thought is "Now I'm going to have to deal with this." Is that fair? Probably not. I would say I'm working on it, but that would be a lie. I'm working on coping with it.

That analogy is imperfect, as are most regarding God. It is a struggle to try to comprehend a being that exists outside of existence. The fact remains that God chose one family as his family. The rest of these families are probably like annoying children on airplanes to him. I'm sure somewhere a professional theologian is shaking their fists at me for even drawing this comparison because God doesn't think, feel, or act like the humans you and I are. The Old Testament, the old covenant, the old promise, represents a promise God made to just one group of people, not all people. You and I may not like that it happened, but that's what happened. Most of the stories of the Old Testament are about God making sure his covenant that he made with this one family is fulfilled. The good news is that there's a reason why the Old Testament is old.

5 // THE DIVINE NATURE

Who is this God? Is he malevolent or benevolent? Is his plan good or evil? How can Abraham or you or I trust him?

Let's imagine that someone approached you and asked to be your best friend. But before you became their friend, they wrote up a contract filled with all the things they were going to do for you. They're going to make you successful, care about what you care about and be in your corner. In the part of the contract that described what was expected of you, it said that this contract was not based on anything having to do with your ability to be a friend to them. You have a part to play, but even if you don't play your part, the terms of the contract stand, and your new friend will fulfill their end of the bargain. They will do their part no matter what you do.

This sounds too good to be true. How can you trust them? You've never spent any time with them. It's like getting a marriage proposal on a blind date. "Let's slow down here and get to know each other first."

Here at the beginning of the story, the start of the Old Testament, there is a covenant. A promise made. Through the rest of the story, God shows us how he holds up his end of the bargain. This story also shows humanity's pathetic attempts and failures to hold up ours. God asked for some simple things out of Abraham and his descendants, but as we are learning, simple ≠ easy.

Let's say this person with a "contract of friendship" directed you to their "friendship reviews" website where you can see what they had done for other people that they had signed contracts with. You see that they are a five-star friend. No fake reviews, all real people. Millions of them. Reviewers would say how time and time again, this person came through for them and was there for them. They would say how there were so many times that the reviewer themselves was a bad friend, but this person did not change who they were because of that. How much confidence would that give you?

The Old Testament represents thousands of years of human history. It shows us many things about ourselves as humans. The greatest thing it shows us is the nature and character of God himself and how he deals with us and our failures. It is God's version of yelp. If you read the Old Testament, you will find time and time again God's attempts to show humanity his plan and get us to play a part.

Richard Dawkins, a renowned biologist says that God is *"arguably the most unpleasant character in all fiction: jealous and proud of it; a petty, unjust, unforgiving control-freak; a vindictive, bloodthirsty ethnic cleanser; a misogynistic, homophobic, racist, infanticidal, genocidal, filicidal, pestilential, megalomaniacal, sadomasochistic, capriciously malevolent bully."* [6] That is a lot of adjectives. You may be inclined to agree with him.

Richard Dawkins is well known for his opposition to the idea of intelligent design. There are many others like him in the science community who believe—with near 100% certainty—that there is no evidence for the existence of God. However, Dawkins himself is more than willing to leave room for the existence of aliens and the microscopic potential that they could have designed life on Earth. Many quantum physicists deny the existence of God vehemently. Yet they will also ask people to believe that time can move backward, objects can exist in two places simultaneously, or that there are multiple universes where every possibility happens. Every possibility that is, except the existence of God.

If God is truly God, then he does not fit neatly into any box or descriptor we could add to him. That's what makes him God. He doesn't have to play by human rules; he created the rules. That's called being sovereign. We may not like it, agree with it or understand it. And we don't get to. We don't make the rules, we don't call the plays, but we're on the field and must play the game as it comes to us. It has been this way for all human history. Even the ideas of good and evil that we hold to are rules and constructs we have created to define morality. How can we apply those to God? God lives outside of all these things that constrain us. Time, space, reality, perhaps even morality. To try to characterize the behavior of God as one way or another according to our standards is foolish after all, if we believe he is truly God. If you're a parent, you are not obligated to explain every decision you make to your kids. If you're a boss, the same holds true. Does God need our consent? Is he accountable to us for his actions? If we believe in a higher power, we should also believe that this higher power functions in ways that extend beyond our ability to perceive them. If we believe in God, we must also understand that is not obligated to explain himself to us. Once we begin to judge God, we see ourselves as god.

Think about this, if God exists outside of time, that means to him that there is no beginning and no end. He sees every moment simultaneously. So he potentially knows, sees, and experiences every moment in history at the same time. God lives like he has one thousand YouTube videos playing in one thousand browser tabs at every moment, and he perceives them concurrently. God lives like he can see the entire feed of humanity on his screen working in real time. That has a lot of implications for our lives that are merely vapor.

The ancient world that Abraham and his family lived in was a lawless and savage place. Acts that would be thought unthinkable today were commonplace then. Infanticide, mass murder and human sacrifice were normal, not exceptions. The rules God created were some of the first of their kind that governed human conduct. That's not a defense of God, that's the facts. He doesn't need me, or us, to defend him after all, if he is God.

From the beginning of human history, **God has had a plan, and he invites us to play a part**. No matter where each one of us falls on the spectrum of religion, there is something in each one of us that recognizes the divine. We know there is something beyond our present experience. Fate, destiny, karma. We may call it something different, but we so badly want to believe that there is more to life than this. Whatever this happens to be.

God, the creator of all of this, says, "yes, there is." He says it to Abraham thousands of years ago, and he says it to us now. And he invites us on a journey.

6 // THE OUTSIDERS

The reason why the Old Testament is important for Gentiles is because it shows us a picture of God with a plan, a purpose for people that he chooses. It shows us the nature and the character of the God who chose Abraham and his family. It shows us God's perspectives, attitudes and actions toward people who he makes promises to. God didn't expect Abraham to go discover this purpose. He invited Abraham on a journey with him and made him a promise. Generation after generation, God revealed more of this promise to Abraham's family. Their role was to take the journey.

Abraham, his family and every human who has ever lived is deeply flawed. God knew that, and he made the covenant anyway. He used every ounce of potential and ability that Abraham's family gave back to him to make that covenant happen.

The caveat for Abraham's family was that to take advantage of the promise, they had to get to know the God that made the promise. Just like Abraham did. That's what the Old Testament shows us: the heart, perspective and actions of God toward humanity.

Who is God to you?

When you think of God, what words come to your mind? Good? Bad? Indifferent? Father? Friend? Creator?

Why do you use the terms you use to refer to God?

For most of us, the answer to that question is based on experience. If we have a positive perspective of God, maybe that's because we had a relative or friend who was a devoted Christian who showed us God's love through their love. Maybe you heard stories about the goodness of God in people's lives growing up.

If we have a bad perspective, that can also be shaped by people in our life. Many people can't see God as a loving father because they were mistreated by their father early in life. Many people have seen terrible things like war, famine and death and can't comprehend a God that would allow such pain. People can also take specific stories and verses from the Bible out of their context and illustrate God's anger and judgment toward people.

The story doesn't end there. There is good news, and the good news is a new covenant that God made with everyone. God decided to go beyond a family of origin and allow anyone who decides to follow him to be part of his covenant family. There's a lot of ground to cover before we get there. Four hundred years' worth.

You probably have a lot of questions. Some can be answered in the Bible. Some of these questions will never be answered. Some questions you will have to answer for yourself. If you start in Genesis and make a dedicated attempt to seek out who God is and how he works, you just might find some answers. You may realize that your life has potential to mean a lot more than you think. This is just the beginning.

There are steps to follow, and the first step is simply getting to know God. Take time and try to understand the design of our world and what that says about the creator. Look at the stories in Scripture and see his character through the way he acts.

Let me give you one question to start. Ask yourself, ask the Old Testament, ask the New Testament, ask people: "What is God like?" The only way to find a satisfactory answer to this question is to decide the answer for yourself in your limited knowledge and experience.

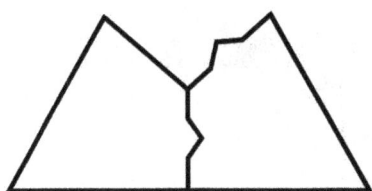

DOT II // US

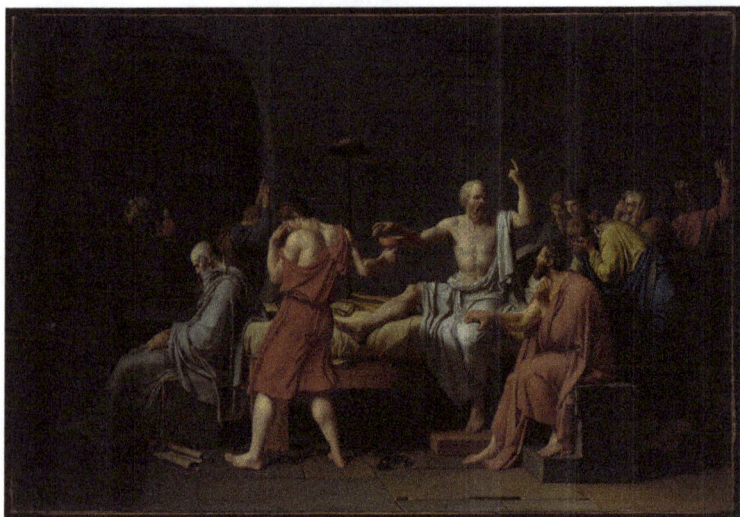

7 // THE SILENCE

Abraham and his family really weren't that special. They were deeply flawed. There were probably better people that God could have made a promise to. In fact, much of the Old Testament seems to be devoted as a chronicle to the mistakes that this family made. But they had one thing: faith.

They may not have believed in themselves, but throughout this collection of books, we see people who fought to believe in the plan that God had for them. That doesn't mean they "set it and forget it." People are people. Wherever we find humanity, we find flaws. No one is the exception. Every person the Old Testament speaks of had issues that would cause them to be unqualified for their role in history. In fact, if they were alive today, some of them would be in jail for a long time.

The Old Testament is thirty-nine books and covers thousands of years of history. The books are filled with history, poetry, law and prophecy. Most of us don't particularly enjoy the law books (Leviticus) or the genealogies (Chronicles). But each one of these books and styles is important and meaningful for different reasons and different groups of people.

Throughout this collection of books, a few things become clear. God has a plan. Humanity plays a role in that plan. To play a role in that plan, people need to get to know the God who created both them and the plan, and God is down for that. People are not good at playing their role—or following or knowing him all that well—and we fail much more than we succeed.

One question to ask when attempting to understand the Old Testament is, "What does this teach us about God?" That is the main purpose of the Old Testament. To know God.

The "newest" book in the Old Testament is the last book, Malachi. Written around 400 BC. When you finish reading the book of Malachi, you're at the end of the Old Testament. In the New Testament we pick up the story in Matthew. We can assume that some things may have happened between Matthew and Malachi, but the story seems to pick up where it left off.

After Malachi, something happened that hadn't happened for a long time: God stopped talking to people. Much has been written about this time in history. It is called the *intertestamental*, or silent period. There is a general belief that there were four hundred years where no one spoke for God because no official Scriptures or text were developed.

These four hundred years in history were characterized by unprecedented human progress:

1. **The rise and fall of the Persian Empire (559-336 BC) //** Founded by Cyrus the Great, Persia was the largest empire in history. The Jewish people were emancipated from exile in Babylon at the end of the Old Testament by Cyrus himself.
2. **The Hellenistic Era (336-31 BC) //** Alexander the Great conquered most of the known world. It was his goal to bring Greek culture to the lands he had conquered; he wished to create a world united by Greek

language and thinking. This was called Hellenization.

3. **The rise of the Roman Empire (31 BC - 476 AD) //**
Julius Caesar rose to power around 45 BC. In 27 BC, Octavius appointed himself "Augustus," which means emperor.

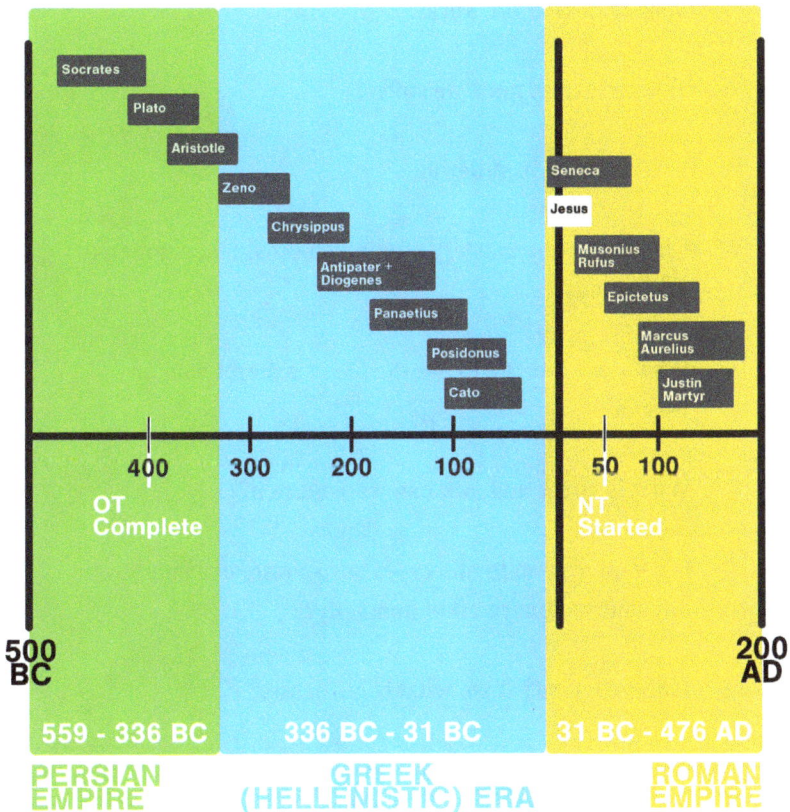

Socrates		
Plato		
Aristotle		
	Zeno	
	Chrysippus	
	Antipater + Diogenes	
	Panaetius	
	Posidonus	
	Cato	Seneca
		Jesus
		Musonius Rufus
		Epictetus
		Marcus Aurelius
		Justin Martyr

400   300   200   100   50 100

OT Complete   NT Started

500 BC   200 AD

559 - 336 BC   336 BC - 31 BC   31 BC - 476 AD

PERSIAN EMPIRE   GREEK (HELLENISTIC) ERA   ROMAN EMPIRE

The Rise of Philosophy

The most significant thing to happen during this silent period in human history was the study of ourselves and how we should live—philosophy. As human beings, we began to look inward and make dedicated attempts to understand and define how we are and how we'd like to be. The ancient philosophers began to ask these questions that we continue to ask today:

△ **Why is there so much distress, anxiety, violence and unhappiness in the world?**

△ **To what extent must we suffer?**

△ **Is there value in suffering?**

△ **Can we develop mastery of our own thoughts, emotions and actions?**

△ **What does it mean to live the life of a moral man or woman?**

△ **What is virtue and how can we acquire it?**

△ **What do we owe to others—to our spouse, our family, our city, our nation, to all of humanity?**

△ **Is there a God? If so, what is his nature?**

△ **Does God care about us?**

△ **What is the good life, and how do we obtain it?**

△ **How can we find happiness?**

It is answers to questions like these that those ancient philosophers attempted to find by stretching human reason to its limits and applying their conclusions within their daily lives—and they found some great answers.

Right before this silent period, in 470 BC, Socrates was born in Athens. He left no writing of his own and is known primarily through those who wrote about him after his death. Socrates, as many of us know, is considered the father of western philosophy. One of the first in a long line of people to ask the question, "Why do we think, feel and act the way we do?"

In the western world, it is believed that he began the study of philosophy.

I mentioned in Chapter two that philosophy, for most of us, seems to be something impractical and disconnected from daily life. That was not the case for Socrates and many of those who came after him. Plato—a student of Socrates—believed that philosophy is unavoidable and inevitable for every person. To be capable of rational thought is to be equipped with all the tools we need to be philosophers. In fact, we become philosophers as soon as our ability to think rationally encounters the world we live in. Every time we make decisions, we are practicing philosophy.

Musonius Rufus said that philosophy is *"nothing else than to search out by reason what is right and proper and by deeds to put it into practice."* [7] In other words, philosophy is how you and I decide we should live our lives.

Cicero said that philosophy teaches us how to be doctors to ourselves.

Socrates, and those who came after him teach us that philosophy is meant to do something very simple: to help us consider and decide the way to live. Any good philosophy is meant to equip us with the tools to live a good life. Philosophy is something we all do. It's something we do almost all the time. We must be philosophers. We already are.

Looking back at the Old Testament through the lens of philosophy, we often find ourselves asking philosophical questions. The same kind of questions that these ancient philosophers would ask: "Why did God choose Abraham and his family?" "Why do bad things happen to innocent people?" And so on.

Without philosophy, we wouldn't care to ask any of these questions. Things would just be as they are.

When we strive to answer the questions, "What do we want out of life?", "How will we measure our life?" and "What is the meaning of our life?" we are actively practicing philosophy.

Whether you realize it or not, when you pursue any form of meaning or happiness, you are developing and living out a "philosophy of life." You are rationally determining your focus and efforts to understand the world as it is and working to create a world you wish to see. Socrates and those who came after him made efforts to provide a template for us to follow and questions for us to answer as we develop our own philosophies of life.

Philosophy is what helps us to create things like core values. It is what guides us to practice empathy and emotional intelligence. Whether we realize it or not, much of our daily lives is guided by the practice of philosophy. Because that's what it is. Practice. Work.

Socrates, and many who came after him were just as concerned with living their philosophy as they were in creating and teaching it. That is the goal we should strive toward, not merely to attempt to think about the deep questions of life but live out our answers to those questions daily.

Once we know God, we can begin to know ourselves. We may begin by asking the question, "What is God like?" The journey doesn't end there. We will eventually find ourselves asking about ourselves. "What am I like, and what do I want to be like?" This is a question of philosophy.

Maybe you're a person who lives a life by default who is more apt to say, "I just am the way that I am." You should realize soon, hopefully now, that you decide how you want to be all the time. No one is "just the way they are." We all can reason, and we use this reason to make decisions on how we live daily. Therefore, we practice philosophy whether we realize it or not.

The question is not whether we will be philosophers or not. The question is whether we will be good or bad philosophers. Will our philosophy be one that we create by design? Or one that we live by default?

Asking ,"What am I like?" will inevitably lead to "What do I want to be like?" and leads us to making decisions about the way to live. When we can decide how we want to be, we are well on our way to living out our philosophy of life.

8 // THE FIRST PIECES

This is a lot of history. We have painted the Old Testament and western philosophy with broad brushstrokes, barely scratching the surface.

We have heard the aphorism "when the student is ready, the teacher appears." This extends to how God deals with humanity. Think sequentially about the progress of human history. From the Stone Age comes Abraham. God asks him to consider the possibility of a divine plan for generations to come. Sure, this thought makes sense to us today. But Abraham was a shepherd living on the backside of the world four thousand-plus years ago. At the time, this was a major development. There is a high likelihood that no one had ever considered something like that in human history until then.

God then takes humanity on a journey for thousands of years so he can demonstrate who he is and how he works from generation to generation. He makes a promise to Abraham and his family and follows through again and again. We know this because these same people chronicled their experiences with God. When we read Scripture, we are reading the stories of people who watched God work in their lives.

Then he went silent. Abraham's family, the Jews, were waiting for God to speak again. They were struggling, just as they always had, to hold up their end of the covenant that Abraham made with God.

Their sense of meaning came from the desire to know God. Their chief goal was to set themselves apart as holy by obeying his laws.

If they could do that—just obey enough—they would accomplish their purpose, an important and foundational piece of God's plan for humanity, but maybe just one piece. Knowing God is the start of the journey. God gave Abraham and his family that one piece, and there were more pieces to come for more people than just Abraham's family.

While the Israelites are making their best efforts to know God, the world kept turning. Along came philosophy. The Gentiles—non-Jewish people—had pantheons of gods that dictated everything from the seasons to omens of childbirth. They weren't considered part of God's family and had no concept of him. They weren't included in the promise.

For most Gentiles, their meaning was not sought in the understanding of the divine but in their understanding of themselves. A piece of God's plan, but just another piece.

St. Augustine, who was a philosopher before he was a Christian and who made important contributions to both philosophy and Christianity, said: *"A person who is a good and true Christian should realize that truth belongs to his Lord, wherever it is found, gathering and acknowledging it even in pagan literature . . ."* [8]

Can philosophy and God work together? Are they meant to?

To understand how to live, it is important for us to understand who God is. His nature and his character. So wouldn't it also be important that we understand ourselves? Does philosophy, something that arose during a time when God "wasn't speaking" play a part in his plan for us?

If all truth is God's truth, could he speak to us without speaking through a prophet? Or a holy book? Can he use both? Most of us would say that God can use whatever he wants; after all, he's God. I am not asserting that ancient philosophers' teachings are equal to Scripture, but God can use whatever he wants to teach us his plan. The rise in philosophy and the silence of God may be a coincidence worth considering.

Philo of Alexandria was a Jewish philosopher who was the first to draw parallels between the Torah and Greek philosophy. Augustine and Jerome referred to Seneca as a Christian writer. Seneca was also considered a saint by some thirteenth-century Catholics. There is an apocryphal story that Paul and Seneca exchanged letters and may have been friends. This was believed to be true until the eighteenth century when researchers began to claim the letters were forgeries. But Acts 17 tells the story of Paul meeting with Stoics and Epicureans, and in Acts 18, Seneca's older brother, Junius Gallio, dismissed charges brought by the Jews against Paul. So, there may be some credence to Paul and Seneca having a relationship. This could be evidence that Christianity and Stoicism have been tied together for a long time.

It is understandable that Christians are often averse to philosophy, as they may be the worst philosophers in modern history. If philosophy is beliefs put into action, one needs to look no further than the reputation of Christians in the modern world to see how well they put their beliefs into action.

Gandhi is quoted as saying *"I like your Christ, but your Christians are so unlike your Christ."* [9]

Does that mean that all Christians do this? Of course not. However, the truth is that most do. Hence the reputation.

So, Christians are bad philosophers. As are most human beings. Most of us struggle with bridging the gap between belief and action. Knowledge is not action. If life is a gym, most of us are out-of-shape people standing on the sidelines critiquing the form of the people attempting to get in shape.

Philosophy is how our minds think and rationalize. We all have philosophies. We don't just need philosophy, we need good philosophy. Because we all need to do a better job of taking what we believe and living by those beliefs. It is essential to understand and decide how we should live. Without it, we cannot hope to live a life that is meaningful. This is philosophy.

The Apostle Paul echoes this in his letter to the Corinthians,

> *"If I had the gift of prophecy, and if I understood all of God's secret plans and possessed all knowledge, and if I had such faith that I could move mountains, but didn't love others, I would be nothing.*
> *|| 1 Corinthians 13:2*

To love someone is not just thinking lovely thoughts toward them. True love is action. We know this.

We have access to more knowledge now than at any time in human history. If we don't act on what we know, not only is this knowledge meaningless, life itself is meaningless. How many of us know what to do, but we don't do it? Knowing how to act is simple. But simple ≠ easy. That's why we need to be intentional about deciding how we should live. Intentional about living out what we believe. Intentional about our philosophy of life.

9 // THE PHILOSOPHY

We have explored the first part of the journey, knowing God, but what does it mean to know ourselves? This is part two of our journey. The philosophers found themselves with a piece, but only a piece. They learned to know themselves but didn't yet know God. For the next few chapters, let's explore what it means for us to know ourselves according to ancient philosophy.

Arguably, the largest and most influential school of philosophy to come out of Greece and spread around the world was Stoicism. It became the dominant school of thought in the Roman Empire. Much of the audience of the New Testament is well versed in Stoic philosophy. Stoicism is the backdrop of the New Testament.

Most often, in the modern world, when we hear the word stoic, we think of a lack of emotion or feeling. While the Stoics believed that the control of one's emotions was important, the term stoic originates from the place that the Stoics met—a stoa. In ancient Greek architecture, a stoa was a covered walkway common for public use. It was under a stoa that the first Stoics gathered.

The components of Stoicism are simple to understand. In fact, much of Stoic philosophy has become common and popular wisdom.

First, you are only responsible for yourself. You cannot control the world, or other people, only yourself. Therefore, your only focus should be on maintaining control of three things: your thoughts, your attitudes and your actions. Everything outside of your control is not worth your effort, time, energy or anxiety. Only focus on what you can personally control.

Sound familiar? Let's revisit dots, lines and triangles.

Think of your life as a triangle. The way you build the triangle is through what you know about God, yourself and the role you decide to play. What lies outside of the triangle is all the things that you can't control. What lies inside of the triangle is all the things that you can control. Your thinking, your attitudes and your actions.

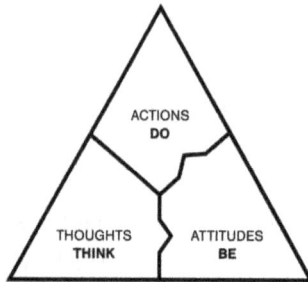

ACTIONS
DO

THOUGHTS
THINK

ATTITUDES
BE

Second, the only way to find any happiness or success is to decide what you value and strive to live those values. The Stoics had four virtues: courage, temperance, justice and wisdom. The only thing that matters at the end of your life is living your virtues, following your true north. Live out your virtues and let the chips fall where they may.

Third, everything outside of your control is not random. It's all part of the plan. There is intelligent design, reason and logic that governs the entire universe. This reasoning, or logos (λόγος), is what separates God, who controls the uncontrollable and creates the plan of the universe, from humanity. The logos is inherently good and should be trusted. God is also the creator of virtue. When we seek to live by virtue, we participate in God's plan for our lives.

To the Stoics, these concepts are easy to understand but difficult to live out. How you live is what matters. Not what you think. You will face adversity and setbacks, and your philosophy is lived out in how you handle those things. A student should learn from a philosopher's life just as much (if not more) as they learn from their teaching.

These three basic concepts form the basis for Stoicism. A philosophy that is simple to understand and demanding to live out. It is just as tough today as it was two thousand years ago. We will explore Stoicism more in the following chapters.

The teaching of philosophy was not centered on classroom instruction but lived experience. Throughout the Roman Empire, parents would send their children to academies: schools of philosophy. Not to learn about reading, writing and arithmetic, but to learn how to live. For generations, these children would become parents and send their own children to these same schools of philosophy. All with the goal of teaching the next generation how to confront the problems they would face.

The rise of philosophy affected everything that came after it. It continues to affect our lives in many ways today. Even though God was silent for four hundred years, generations of people learned to live meaningful lives. Again, this is just one piece.

10 // THE THINKING

"Very little is needed to make a happy life; it is all within yourself, in your way of thinking." // **Marcus Aurelius**

I once heard a story of a hunter who bought a bird dog, the only one of its kind in the world. This bird dog could walk on water. He couldn't believe his eyes when he saw this miracle. At the same time, he was very pleased that he could show off his new acquisition to his friends, so he invited a friend to go duck hunting. After some time, they shot a few ducks, and the man ordered his dog to run and fetch the birds. All day long, the dog ran on water and kept fetching the birds. The owner was expecting a comment or a compliment about his amazing dog but never got one. As they were returning home, he asked his friend if he had noticed anything unusual about his dog. The friend replied, "Yes, in fact, I did notice something unusual. Your dog can't swim.

How we perceive things is often more important than the
things themselves.

What are you in control of? Really think about it. If you really spend some time on it, you'll probably end up with three things, or some variation of them.

- ▲ **My thinking:** The way I choose to think about anything and everything.

- ▲ **My attitude:** The way I choose to respond to my feelings about anything and everything.
- ▲ **My actions:** What I choose to do about anything and everything.

What can you not control?
- ▲ What people think
- ▲ What people think of me
- ▲ How people behave
- ▲ How well someone else does their job
- ▲ How rude people are
- ▲ Other people's habits
- ▲ Other people's success
- ▲ How well other people listen to you
- ▲ How much someone behaves the way you want them to
- ▲ What other people fear or find stressful
- ▲ Everything else

You and I only possess control of our thoughts, attitude and action. But what do we spend most of our thoughts, attitudes and actions on? What do we base our thoughts, attitudes and actions on?

If we're honest, we would say that much of the time, we allow the list of what we can't control to control the list we can control. Our thinking is shaped by what other people think. Our attitudes are determined by the attitudes of others, how they make us feel, or our instinctive emotional responses to what we experience. Our actions are based on what other people do or what makes us feel comfortable.

We live as if we are powerless to the things around us. Much of what we think, feel and do seems to be dictated by circumstances far beyond our control. Therefore, we feel stuck in life, not able to move forward in any meaningful way until our circumstances change.

We find ourselves powerless to change our circumstances. We are who we are because of where we grew up, who are parents were, or whether our boss or teacher likes us.

We find ourselves in snowballs of negative outcomes, negative actions, negative attitudes and negative thoughts. These things build on top of each other almost infinitely. A negative thought becomes a negative attitude, a negative attitude becomes a negative action. A negative action leads to negative outcomes. How can we stop the snowball?

Begin with your thinking, your perceptions.

We are not always in control of the situations that we may find ourselves in. We are always in control of how we choose to view those situations. What makes a situation good or bad? The situation itself or your perspective of it?

"This event happened, and this event is bad" are two statements in one. "This happened" is an objective statement of fact. An event took place. "This is bad" is a subjective statement based on our perspective.

Ryan Holiday, in his book *The Obstacle is the Way*, uses this analogy.

Insert your life event here:

           _____ happened and it is _____ (good/bad).

There are a lot of people who go through difficulties in life and make the statement, "This isn't supposed to be this way." It's not supposed to be that way according to what? One of the easiest ways to know that you aren't in control of a situation is if that situation isn't the way you want it to be. Obviously, if you were in control, you would make the situation go the way you wanted. Instead of saying how a situation is "supposed to be," it is more worth our efforts to say, "here's how I'm going to respond to this situation."

In psychology, this is called the framing effect. People often will make different choices based on how they perceive or see a situation presented.

How does framing work? Are you a glass half full or a glass half empty person? That is framing—how you interpret a situation presented to you.

Let's say you need surgery, the first doctor who you speak to says that you will have a 90 percent chance of surviving the operation. The second doctor you speak with tells you that you have a 10 percent chance of dying. These are the same odds but different ways of framing them.

The situations we face in life are often not pretty, but how we decide to see them can make all the difference. The way we decide to interpret and think about what happens to us will determine our response to those things.

"Another person will not do you harm unless you wish it; you will be harmed at just that time at which you take yourself to be harmed." [10]
// Epictetus

"It is not how the wrong is done that matters, but how it is taken." [11]
// Seneca

This does not mean that we pretend that there is no problem or setback. It means that we choose to see the setback or problem as an opportunity to move forward. In fact, it is the only way that we can.

Robert Cumming, a distinguished art critic, stood in London's National Gallery studying a fifteenth-century painting by Filippino Lippi. This painting, titled *The Virgin and Child* with Saints Jerome and Dominic featured Mary holding the infant Jesus on her lap with Saints Dominic and Jerome kneeling nearby. Art critics like Robert Cumming were often puzzled by this painting. There could be no doubting Lippi's skill, his use of color or composition. But the proportions of the picture seemed slightly wrong. The hills in the background seemed skewed and misplaced. Jerome and Dominic were kneeling at uncomfortable angles. Mary seemed to be staring inexplicably at the ground.

Cumming was the first art critic to realize something special about this painting. It suddenly occurred to him that the problem might be one of perspective. The painting had never been intended to come anywhere near a gallery. Lippi's painting had been commissioned to hang in a place of prayer.

The dignified critic dropped to one knee in the public gallery before the painting. He suddenly saw what generations of art critics had missed. From his new vantage point, he found himself gazing up at a perfectly proportioned piece of art. The foreground had moved naturally to the background, while the saints settled into realistic positions. Mary now looked intently and kindly directly at him instead of the ground.

It was not the perspective of the painting that had been wrong all these years, it was the perspective of the people looking at it. The painting only came alive to those on their knees in prayer.

The first, and most important, thing you can control is your thinking. Your perspective on yourself, your life, your problems, and everything else will make things better, keep them the same or, God forbid, make them worse. Your thinking, and thus your perspective about any situation—good or bad—is the greatest predictor of the outcome of that situation. Even more than the facts of the situation. Yes, there are facts. Objectively, things do happen to us. But there are also perceptions. Subjectively, the way we think about those facts is what matters most. Not the facts themselves.

Put on glasses that have blue lenses. Now look at a lemon. What color is the lemon? It is yellow. A lemon isn't going to change its color. But with blue-lensed glasses, the lemon looks green to us. That's the power of your thinking, your perspective.

Growing up with a dad like mine, I don't remember a time where I wasn't surrounded with questions and thoughts like these. One of the questions that I heard him repeat often, and continue to hear him ask today, is: "Who taught you to think the way you think?"

Ask yourself that question. Who taught you to think the way you think? Why do you see the world the way you do? Where does your perspective come from?

Every great philosopher has a teacher. Aristotle had Plato; Plato had Socrates. Jacob had Isaac; Isaac had Abraham. One of the best steps you can take toward your life being meaningful is to find someone who can teach you how to think better.

So, who taught you to think the way that you think? Who should be teaching you to think better? Can you think better? Can you have a better perspective than the one you currently have? Of course you can. The real question is: How will you acquire it?

Another question that I've heard my dad ask is what he calls the "effectiveness question." That question is simple. *"How's that working out for you?"*

This is the question that we all can use to measure the effectiveness of any philosophy that we observe. Someone may be a great learner, they may have had deep and meaningful experiences, but does their life, their actions, reflect the truths they speak?

Does your personal trainer follow their same diet and exercise plan with results? Has the person who is teaching you how to parent raised great kids? Does the individual who is telling you how to treat your spouse have a great marriage?

When weighing any philosophy or way of thinking being presented, ask the effectiveness question. "How is that working out for you?"

If it is not working in the life of the teacher, it won't work in the life of the student.

The Stoics teach us that we have the power at any moment to choose to maintain the right perspective. They say that through their own lived experiences. Zeno was shipwrecked and lost everything. Seneca was sentenced to death. Musonius Rufus was exiled from his home. Marcus Aurelius was emperor during a plague that is believed to have killed 10 percent of the Roman Empire—five million people—in a fifteen-year period. Justin Martyr became the first martyr for his faith.

But none of them allowed their negative experiences to transform their perspective negatively.

Zeno said, *"I made a prosperous voyage when I suffered a shipwreck."*[12] He founded the Stoic school that became the primary school of philosophy in the Roman Empire. Musonius Rufus was so respected that he was the only philosopher allowed in the city of Rome for a time. Marcus Aurelius is one of the five good emperors who presided over the Roman Empire's greatest days. Justin Martyr was one of the first Christian apologists and is venerated as a saint in the Catholic Church, Anglican Church, the Eastern Orthodox Church and the Oriental Orthodox Churches.

It's one thing to experience something; it's another thing entirely to allow that experience to make you think negatively. You might not be able to control your situation, but you can control your thinking. Don't let your thinking be ruined by your situation. This is what it means to control our thinking.

"We suffer more in imagination (perception) than reality."

// Seneca

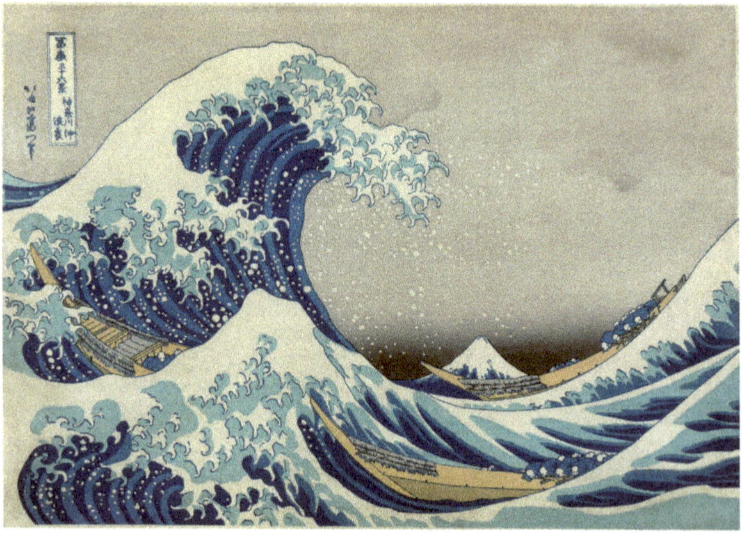

11 // THE BEING

"A man is as unhappy as he has convinced himself he is." // **Seneca**

In Stoic philosophy, there is a sequence. How you think leads to the next step. That next step is your attitude. Your state of being. Once we've considered our thinking, we must consider our attitude.

Why do you feel the way that you feel? Good and bad? What makes you feel positive feelings? What makes you feel negative feelings? The way most of us answer these kinds of questions sounds something like, "When good things happen, I feel good. When bad things happen, I feel bad."

Most people don't realize they are in control of what they think about. Therefore, most people don't realize they are in control of their attitude. What creates your feelings and attitudes? It is your thinking.

If you want to understand your attitude, start with how you are choosing to think about that thing.

Prior to World War II, **Victor Frankl** was one of Vienna's most distinguished doctors. He had a wife, family, prestige and success. The Nazi nightmare changed it all. He spent several years in concentration camps performing slave labor and inhuman tasks. Frankl survived the Nazi horrors and in his book *Man's Search for Meaning*, he describes the horrors and hope of life in a concentration camp. He said that the last of the human freedoms is "to choose one's attitude in any given set of circumstances, to choose one's own way." [13]

"Keep in mind that what injures you is not people who are rude or aggressive but your opinion that they are injuring you." [14]

// **Epictetus**

"Choose not to be harmed and you won't feel harmed. Don't feel harmed and you haven't been." [15]

// **Marcus Aurelius**

We've all heard it, "when life gives you lemons, you make lemonade." That's a good sentiment, but it takes work to turn lemons into lemonade. It doesn't just happen. I'm convinced that some people believe the more upset they become, and the louder they complain about the lemons, the faster they'll turn into lemonade.

Without lemons, I wouldn't be able to make lemonade. What's bad about a lemon? The way we decide to see and feel about lemons is what's bad, not the lemons themselves.

Difficulty and struggle are common to all of humanity. All of us will face challenges in life. Setbacks, struggles, problems. What's the worst thing that could happen to us when faced with difficulty? Most of us would say the difficulty itself. Events that are outside of our control can and will happen to us. The worst thing that could happen would be if we experienced a setback and lost control of our attitude at the same time. Then we would have two problems and one of them is our fault, and unnecessary.

The problem is still the problem. The event is still the event. The "problem" will still be there no matter how we feel about it. One choice makes our lives a little bit easier: the choice of our attitude. How we respond to how we feel about the problem.

Of course, like most things, simple ≠ easy. It's easy to understand that we can and should control our emotions and attitudes well. Emotions are hard to predict and understand, and attitude is much more than emotion. Most of the time, we need to have a certain attitude and set aside our emotions.

In aviation, an attitude is the orientation of a plane relative to Earth. In other words, an attitude reading tells us the direction a plane is pointing. Regardless of the conditions it finds itself in.

"It is your attitude, more than your aptitude, that will determine your altitude." [16]   **|| Zig Ziglar**

This is true in aviation, and it also seems to be true in life. The direction we decide to point will determine where we go. If we believe something to be good, it will be good. If we believe something to be bad, it will be bad.

Dr. Martin Seligman in his book, *Learned Optimism*, describes a study that he conducted. He found that negative people get sick more often, are divorced more frequently, and raise kids who get in more trouble. [17]

Dr. Seligman even found that negative people make less money. In one long-term study of 1,500 people, 83% of the people took their jobs because they believed they could make lots of money. Only 17% of them took their jobs because they had a positive attitude about their jobs. Twenty years later, the two groups had produced 101 millionaires. The amazing thing is, only one of those millionaires came from the 83%, but 100 of them came from the 17%. [18]

According to Dr. Seligman, over 70% of those millionaires never went to college. And over 70% of those who became CEOs graduated in the bottom half of their class. [19]

How does our attitude differ from our emotions? Is "being positive" the same as being happy? There is much debate regarding human emotions. Some people say that our emotions are always within our control and we can choose how we feel. Some people assert that our emotions are instinctive responses that we are incapable of dictating. This is like a fight-or-flight response. Whether we can control our emotions or not, we can always control our attitudes. Our attitude is our will. It is our ability to restrain and control our emotions and impulses. Whether you believe you are in control of your emotions or not, you are always in control of what you do with your emotions. And what you do with your emotions constitutes your attitude.

What is a positive attitude?

Cheetahs are the fastest land animals in the world. They can run up to seventy-five mph and can go from zero to sixty mph in about 3.4 seconds. However, science tells us that if a cheetah ran for more than thirty seconds straight, it would die from exhaustion.

Usain Bolt is the fastest human being in history. In 2009, he ran a 9.58-second hundred-meter dash. Which equates to around a 27.8 mph top speed.

It is likely that no matter what humanity does, we will not ever be able to run faster than a cheetah without the assistance of technology. Our biology prevents it. But pretty much every human being that can run, can run thirty seconds straight without dying.

In 2005, Dean Karnazes ran 350 miles without stopping even to sleep. He ran for eighty hours and forty-four minutes without a break. Over these 350 miles, he averaged a thirteen-minute mile.

The human body is not built for speed. It is built for endurance. Biologists say that one of the key things that makes human beings the dominant species on the earth is our ability to endure an untold variety of challenges, climates and circumstances. Endurance athletes speak about "runner's high" or second wind during lengthy or intense exercise. Researchers say this happens because when we experience intense exertion, our nervous system floods our body with endorphins. These endorphins produce feelings of happiness, euphoria and decrease anxiety and feelings of pain. The pain of pushing through exercise is what causes our body to release endorphins that release the pain. Endurance can produce positive feelings.

If endurance through physical pain leads to a positive result, why couldn't the same thing happen emotionally? Our attitude is what gives us the ability to endure difficult situations and emotions. Being positive is not about smiling our way through things; it's about believing our way through things. How can endurance be an attitude? Patience. Patience is your capacity to accept or tolerate delay, trouble, or suffering without getting angry or upset. To practice the attitude of endurance, we must practice patience. If we are enduring something, it's because we think we can get through it. If we are patient in the midst of a process, we are having a good attitude while the process is taking place. Think about this, to a small child a month is an eternity. For most adults a month passes rather quickly. As we grow older, our relationship to time changes and we are more patient with the passage of time. A good measure of our maturity is how patient we are. Many people may look mature, and they may even act mature, but when the time comes for patience or endurance in their life, they wither. The greatest attitude we can have is patience. You and I may feel like quitting, but that's just a feeling. Our feelings should be secondary to our attitude. Call it grit, resilience or staying power. Patience is not a feeling, it's a deliberate response to how we feel.

"It's not necessary for all men to be great in action. the greatest and most sublime power is patience." [20] // **Horace Bushnell**

A human being's greatest physical strength is their ability to endure and their greatest emotional strength is the ability to be patient.

Patience is not passive. Patience, just like endurance is knowing that if you can persevere and not quit, you will prevail. There are times where we feel like we are in a fight and we have to win. In ancient Greece when they trained armies, they wouldn't train them to be skilled at battle. They trained them to endure the fight. In ancient warfare, standing your ground and "looking spears in the face" was the greatest predictor of victory in warfare. The ability to mentally endure a battle was ten times more important than the skill to fight.

The strength of ancient Greek warriors was not their fighting ability but their readiness to face hardship and danger. As the Spartan poet Tyrtaeus put it, [21]

> *This is a common benefit for the state and all the people: when a man stands firm in the front without ceasing, and, making his heart and soul endure, banishes all thought of shameful flight, encouraging his neighbour with words. This is a man good in war; he quickly turns the waves of enemy spears, and stems the tide of battle with his will.*

A good warrior is not one who kills the most, or who outmatches their enemies in skill. A good warrior endures in the heat of battle. A good warrior encourages others to endure. The difference between a good warrior and a bad one is the amount of time they are prepared to stay in the battle before they retreat.

In the Iliad, Homer talks about Ajax, the son of King Telamon. Ajax is described like a tower. He never moves, never retreats, and allows others to rally around him. In battle, Ajax leads his army into battle with only a defensive weapon, a shield made of seven cow hides covered in bronze. His greatest strength is his ability to outlast the attacks of his enemies. Homer tells us that Odysseus and Achilles would surge forward in battle and force the enemy back. The ideal hero is not someone who can beat their opponent in a fight but someone who shows courage and inspires courage in others like Ajax. This was not just Homer's ideal, this was true for many leaders in ancient war. And it's still true today.

We see this clearly when we turn to the legendary warriors of actual history. Authors like Herodotos and Plutarch tell stories of heroes who are always heroically brave but never heroically skilled. They tell stories of people like Sophanes, who challenged his enemy to charge at him. He did so only after placing an iron anchor into the ground and chaining himself to it to face the onslaught.[22] Socrates himself was described by Epictetus as a brave warrior.

"[Socrates] was the first to go out as a soldier, when it was necessary, and in war he exposed himself to danger most unsparingly." [23]

// Epictetus

A legendary warrior in ancient Greece was one who had proven themselves brave when it mattered—a person who endured. A warrior was someone who could serve as an example to others, who also needed to be brave. Facing this kind of person in battle would be terrifying. Fighting alongside them would be inspiring.

Having a good attitude isn't about being happy or only experiencing good things. Having a good attitude is about staying in the fight. It has nothing to do with your skills, feelings, or even fear. We must tame our fear when it really matters, stare our enemy in the face and hold the line no matter what. The greatest enemies that most of us will face are our own negative emotions. If you stay in the fight, it's because you believe you can still win. That's a positive attitude. That's real patience.

"If it's endurable, then endure it. If it's not endurable ... then stop complaining. Your destruction will mean its end as well." [24]

// Marcus Aurelius

The direction you decide to point the plane will determine if you go up or down. Most of the time, success is just about getting on the other side of the obstacle. It's about being willing to endure the fight, stand like a tower and not run away. The only way out is through. So if you're going through hell, keep going.

""Is a world without pain possible? Then don't ask the impossible." [25]

// Marcus Aurelius

Many of us believe that there will come a day where we face no difficulties. We live with a belief that our lives are somehow supposed to get easier. One day, we will enter a magical land where nothing is hard and we always feel good. We end up inadvertently setting this imaginary land as a goal for our lives.

There's a Haitian proverb: *"Dèyè mòn, gen mòn"*

Behind mountains, there are mountains.

You are made to win. Your win will be determined by your ability to endure. Your ability to endure will be determined by the attitude you choose to have. Have the attitude of patience. You can and will climb this mountain you are facing. Once you climb it, you will see the next mountain you have to climb. Understand that you are built to do this, created for it. Passing one test just means you get to take the next one. Every challenge you face is meant to help your life get better. The only way to win in life is to continue to climb your mountains and do it with a smile on your face. We can smile because we understand that we were created to do this. It's not supposed to be easy; the race is hard and long. We should see all adversity as an opportunity to practice a good attitude. The difficulty you face is meant to teach you to endure. Whatever you're in, commit to stay in it. If you stay in it, you'll win. If you stay in it, you inspire everyone around you. Just like the heroes of ancient Greece. Staying in this fight will take everything you have.

"...regard all adversity as a training exercise." [26] // **Seneca**

Do not let your emotions cloud your state of being. Your being, your attitude, is always up to you no matter the circumstances you face.

It's hard, yes. But who said it wasn't supposed to be? The truth is, it's going to be hard either way. Hard is a guarantee. Don't make molehills into mountains, make mountains into molehills.

Being your Best is hard.
Being your normal is hard.

Making wise decisions is hard.
Making bad decisions is hard.

Being in shape is hard.
Being out of shape is hard.

Losing weight is hard.
Being fat is hard.

Working out is hard.
Being weak is hard.

Being disciplined is hard.
Being lazy is hard.

Getting out of your comfort zone is hard.
Staying in your comfort zone is hard.

Starting a business is hard.
Working for someone else is hard.

Making a lot of money is hard.
Making a little bit of money is hard.

Being rich is hard.
Being poor is hard.

Having great relationships is hard.
Having bad relationships is hard.

Having friends is hard.
Having no friends is hard.

Fighting for your marriage is hard.
Divorce is hard.

Having a lot of things is hard.
Having nothing is hard.

Living on purpose is hard.
Living off purpose is hard.

Doing life God's way is hard.
Doing life your own way is hard.

Everything is hard!
Choose your hard! [27]

// Keith Craft

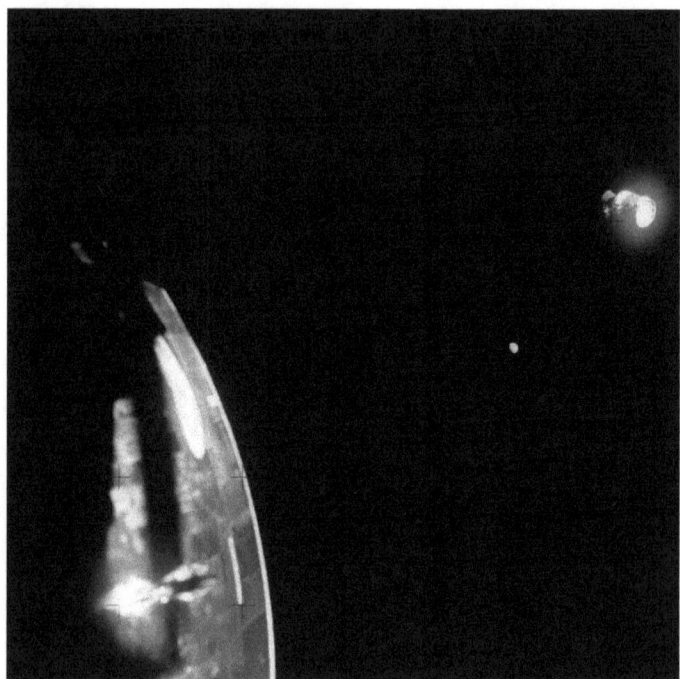

12 // THE DOING

Think of something good you have done. Why did you do it?

Think of something bad you have done. Why did you do it?

My favorite reason for doing anything has been "because I felt like it." When I was young, the way I felt dictated almost every action that I took. So much so that it spawned a philosophy for my dad:

"It's easier to act your way into a feeling than feel your way into an action."

Most of us wait to act until we feel like it. We will eat healthy when we feel like it. We'll go to the gym when we feel like it. We'll treat people with respect when we feel like it. We will rise to the challenges we face when we feel like it.

If you wait to feel like it, you'll probably realize the same thing I did: that feeling doesn't come all too often. That is why controlling our perspective and attitude matters so much. If I don't control those things, my actions will also be out of control.

My teacher and father Keith Craft teaches it this way:

Think + Be + Do = Have

How you think + your state of being (your attitude) + what you do = what you have in life. Always. It's immutable, eternal knowledge. What you have in your life right now is a direct result of your actions. Your actions are a direct result of your attitude. Your attitude is a direct result of your thinking and perspective.

Your thinking, being and doing are the only things that lie within your triangle of control. Worrying about anything outside of that is futile.

Of course this makes sense in theory, but what makes this difficult to do? The same thing that makes having the right perspective and attitude difficult. Much about our life lies outside of our control. We may approach the events of our life with a certain plan and idea of what we will do and how we will respond, but life always has surprises in store for us. Some surprises are pleasant, many are unpleasant.

"Everyone has a plan until they get punched in the mouth." [28]

// Mike Tyson

Apollo 13, the third mission to attempt to land on the moon had run into a life-threatening issue 203,980 miles from help. A faulty wire caused one of their two oxygen tanks to explode, and the other began to rapidly lose oxygen. These two tanks gave the crew both oxygen and power, one was now gone, and the other was leaking.

They were so close to the moon, right above it. They could see their objective. However, this accident meant two things. The mission they planned was over, and their new mission was to figure out a way to get back to Earth alive.

Time was short and there seemed to be no options for their survival. The command module–the Odyssey–designed to support three men for their journey to the moon and reentry to Earth's atmosphere was no longer viable. The Aquarius, the lunar module, designed to land on the moon was their only option.

They frantically worked to boot Aquarius up in less time than designed. However, Aquarius didn't have a heat shield to survive the drop back to Earth, so the astronauts had to do everything they could to shut down the Odyssey as quickly as possible to conserve power for splashdown. They also had to figure out how the Aquarius, which was designed to support two men for two days, could support three men for four days.

In the Aquarius, the crew found enough oxygen to breathe, but challenges kept coming. They had to figure out a way to filter carbon dioxide, survive with very little water, make precise reentry calculations with very little functional equipment, in perpetual 38°F temperatures.

All three men survived, but they never made it to the moon. Most of us today wouldn't consider this mission a failure, even though it didn't meet its initial objectives. Why? Because the goals changed based on things outside of the astronauts' control.

A NASA flight controller was asked after this,

"Weren't there times when everybody, or at least a few people, just panicked?" [29]

His answer was "No, when bad things happened, we just calmly laid out all the options, and failure was not one of them."

In the movie, we see people rushing around in a panic trying to solve the problems that were being presented. This was not the case. The mission changed and so did their actions. Their actions were not reactionary and wild. They were logical, rational and calm—no matter the circumstances. [30]

When we are given the proper amount of time to prepare and plan, we can ensure that we have proper perspective, good attitudes and, therefore, right actions. The problem, however, is what we do when things don't go according to plan. When things don't go our way, what do we do? What should we do?

The Stoics would counsel us to have an even mind—stability and composure—regardless of the circumstance. Don't be disturbed by your experiences or by exposure to pain, emotions or other things that may cause other people to lose their composure.

The Greek Stoics called it apatheia, the Roman Stoics called it equanimity. Justin Martyr, Clement of Alexandria and Saint Ignatius considered it a significant aspect of Christianity. Equanimity is calmness that comes with the absence of irrational or extreme emotions. Not the loss of feelings, but the loss of harmful feelings.

This doesn't mean we resolve ourselves to the way things are. We do not say, "Que sera sera." Whatever will be will be. Equanimity is not passivity; it is giving your best to make things happen, and then remaining composed when things don't go your way.

Think about what worries you. What causes you anxiety? What interferes with your composure? It often turns out that the things that worry us the most lie the farthest outside of our control. What can you do about what worries you? Most of the time, we can do nothing. So why worry? Why lose our control? Why should we allow the things we can't control to affect what we can?

Life is a fight with no rules

Pankration was a Greek Olympic fighting sport with hardly any rules. The goal of pankration was to do whatever you could to get your opponent to quit. Pankratists would bite, kick, gouge, box and choke each other. The contest would last until you, or your opponent, submitted or died. In fact, there is a record of someone named Arrhichion of Phigalia winning the pankration competition at the Olympic Games despite being dead. His opponent had locked him in a chokehold and Arrhichion, desperate to loosen it, broke his opponent's toe (some records say his ankle). The opponent nearly passed out from pain and submitted. As the referee raised Arrhichion's hand, it was discovered that he had died from the choke-hold. His body was crowned with an olive wreath and returned to Phigalia as a hero.[31] Arrhichion shows us that if you don't quit, even if you die, you can be a winner.

Panaetius describes life as a pankration contest:

The life of men who pass their time in the midst of affairs, and who wish to be helpful to themselves and to others, is exposed to constant and almost daily troubles and sudden dangers. To guard against and avoid these, one needs a mind that is always ready and alert, such as the athletes have who are called 'pancratists.' For just as they, when called to the contest, stand with their arms raised and stretched out, and protect their head and face by opposing their hands as a rampart; and as all their limbs, before the battle has begun, are ready to avoid or to deal blows—so the spirit and mind of the wise man, on the watch everywhere and at all times against violence and wanton injuries, ought to be alert, ready, strongly protected, prepared in time of trouble, never flagging in attention, never relaxing its watchfulness, opposing judgment and forethought like arms and hands to the strokes of fortune and the snares of the wicked, lest in any way a hostile and sudden onslaught be made upon us when we are unprepared and unprotected.[32]

What does this have to do with equanimity? Living life is not a passive activity. We must be ready to live. Life is conflict. We should be willing to embrace the conflict and struggle that comes with our existence. Our life is not just our thinking or attitude, it is our action. Paul encourages Timothy in this same way in 1 Timothy 6:12 to "fight the good fight of faith." You may not have chosen the fight, but it is here. What do you plan to do? Is life something that is happening to you or are you willing to act? You're going to get punched in the mouth, it's a guarantee. You can't avoid it. Are you prepared for it? What are you going to do when it happens?

Living a good life is not a result of finding comfort, decreasing our difficulty, and shrinking from challenges. A good life is had by one who embraces challenges head on and acts on those challenges with equal force. Do you feel like you're in over your head? Good. Now it's time to learn to swim.

"It is the power of the mind to be unconquerable." [33]   **// Seneca**

We should not live our lives to fight everyone and everything in our path. Our goal is not to add to the chaos. Our goal is to control ourselves amid chaos. Our focus is to learn how to control only the things that we can control. That means we do not run from a battle, but we also don't go looking for them. We must be disciplined, pursue equanimity and maintain our composure at all times. Life can feel like an onslaught, and if we are prepared to act as if it is, we won't be caught unprepared and unprotected. We will be able to respond calmly and rationally.

In the *Haggadah*, the Jewish people are reminded every year on Passover that they should view themselves as if they personally escaped slavery in Egypt. They do this as a reminder of the goodness of God and the pain and difficulty that life often brings. Life can be painful, but God is always good. This too shall pass. Don't let the situation dictate your response. Situations and circumstances may change, but we must maintain equanimity.

Have the perspective that life will deal its blows. Live with the attitude that you can endure. Act with equanimity and keep your composure. If you do this, you will always find a way forward. God has a plan. You will have a good life. Act like it.

When we live this way, we will have a great life. Why? Because what we have in life will not be based on what we can't control. We will control our thoughts, our attitudes and our actions and have a great life.

Think + Be + Do = Have

13 // THE VIRTUES

As we've decided, our goal is to live a life of meaning. To make an impact. We want to do what is right; we want to do what is good. So how do we decide what is good?

We mostly think that the things we want are good things. But good things are not always good for us. Junk food is an example. Fried chicken is delicious. That makes us want it because it tastes good. Isn't fried chicken unhealthy? Yes, that makes us not want it because it's bad for us. We want it, because it tastes good, but we shouldn't want it, because it's bad for us.

It may seem that things that are painful are bad because we often think pain is bad. But many things that are painful are not things we should avoid. Working out is often painful. Therefore, is it bad? Working out also increases my health and quality of life, so it's good. So, what is painful is not always bad. Life, like food and exercise, is often confusing, as you can see. Things that feel good are sometimes bad. Things that feel bad are sometimes good. Salad tastes so bad, how could it possibly be good for us?

How do we know we are doing what is good and not bad? How do we know we are doing the right thing and not the wrong thing? We are often counseled to look at what prevailing culture establishes as acceptable and use that as a template. Alas, we know the folly of this. For a long period of human history, slavery was not just acceptable, it was seen as good. Racism in the form of segregation was also seen as ethical and moral at one time. There is much about our world today that may be seen as good and desirable now, but that doesn't make these things so.

We see this dilemma play out in professional sports too. Lance Armstrong cheated his way to seven Tour dé France cycling titles. While competing, he stated vehemently that he never cheated. Shortly after his career was over, in an exclusive interview with Oprah, he admitted to doping throughout his cycling career. During his admission, he said that it didn't feel like he was cheating because everyone he knew was doping. The culture created his standard for goodness..

*""Everyone cheats," s*aid White Sox manager **Ozzie Guillen** in 2005. *"If you don't get caught, you're a smart player. If you get caught, you're cheating."* [34]

Many athletes who get caught doping use the excuse that everyone is doing it. We do too. If we are honest with ourselves, we would admit that what we see as acceptable—or even good—is based on what those around us see as acceptable. This is an impotent way to live. We teach our children that the road to mediocrity is following the crowd while justifying our actions because "everyone else is doing it." Even worse, there are many people who live life with a "no good deed goes unpunished" mentality. Where they may as well be selfish, unkind, or evil because they are going to be mistreated anyway.

How do we avoid this? We are not immune to what caused Lance Armstrong or many before and after him to fall. We are human just like them.

The only way to ensure that our thoughts, attitudes and actions are right and good is to make sure we have a true north on the compass of life. We must know this true north and always keep it in front of us.

What matters most in your life? You may know what you want in life, but how do you plan to get there? We know that we should have the right perspective, attitudes and actions, but what does it mean for them to be "right"? How can you know you are doing the right thing? Especially when it seems you are swimming upstream and everyone else is headed in the opposite direction?

The Stoics claimed that the reason to control our thoughts, attitudes and actions was because all that mattered was living a life of virtue. Culture, ideologies, ethics and even morals change. But our virtues can withstand the onslaught of life. True nobility lies in the pursuit of what is good and right. What is good and right can only be defined in the context of our virtues.

The Stoic virtues are:

- ▲ **Wisdom** - The ability to transcend good and evil. To differentiate between what is good and what is best and choose what is best.
- ▲ **Courage** - The power to have equanimity, resiliency and bravery in the face of danger and fear.
- ▲ **Temperance** - The ability to practice moderation, self-control and self-discipline.
- ▲ **Justice** - Doing what is right and fair for others first, and ourselves second.

The Stoics believed that they would do good as long as they strived to live by these four things. "Rightness" is a matter of living by virtue, not doing what seems pleasant in the moment or culturally acceptable.

The way to be truly good is to choose a life of principle. To live a life of virtue.

THE WAY TO LIVE 1.0.1 // DOT II // US

In the early 1900s, Al Capone virtually owned Chicago and was one of the most famous people in America. He was notorious for entangling the Windy City in everything from bootlegged alcohol and prostitution to murder.

Al Capone had a lawyer nicknamed "Easy Eddie." He was Capone's lawyer for a good reason: Eddie was very good at what he did. In fact, Eddie's skill at legal maneuvering kept Capone out of jail for a long time. Eddie was paid very well, and his estate was so large it filled a Chicago city block.

Eddie enjoyed his life and didn't think much about the activities of Al Capone and the mobsters he represented. After all, he was just their lawyer, he didn't do any of the things that the Mob did. He was a good man who worked with bad people. At least, that's how he justified it. Eddie had a son he loved dearly and used every resource he had to provide his son with every opportunity.

Despite his involvement with organized crime, Eddie resolved to teach his son right from wrong. Eddie wanted him to be a better man than he was. Yet with all his wealth and influence, Eddie realized that there were two things he couldn't give his son: he couldn't pass on a good name and he couldn't set a good example.

One day, Easy Eddie reached a difficult decision. Wanting to right the wrongs he had done, he decided he would go to the authorities and tell the truth about Capone and the Mob, clean up his tarnished name, and live a life his son could follow. To do this, he would have to testify against the Mob. The cost would be great, but he testified.

On November 8, 1939, Easy Eddie's life would end in a blaze of gunfire on a lonely Chicago street.

Three years later, on February 20, 1942, Lt. Cmdr. Butch O'Hare was a fighter pilot assigned to the aircraft carrier Lexington in the South Pacific.

One day, his entire squadron was sent on a mission. After he was airborne, Butch looked at his fuel gauge and realized he would not have enough fuel to complete his mission and get back to his ship. His flight leader told him to return to the carrier. Reluctantly, he dropped out of formation and headed back to the fleet. As he was returning to his carrier, he noticed an entire squadron of Japanese aircraft speeding their way toward the American fleet.

All the American fighters that would normally defend the fleet were gone on a mission, and the fleet was defenseless. He couldn't reach his squadron and bring them back in time to save the fleet, nor could he warn the fleet of the approaching danger. There was only one thing to do. He must somehow divert the oncoming aircraft. Laying aside all thoughts of personal safety, he dove into the formation of Japanese planes.

Wing-mounted .50-caliber guns blazed as he attacked one surprised enemy plane after another. Butch wove in and out of the now broken formation and fired until all his ammunition was spent. Undaunted, he continued the assault. He dove at the planes, trying to clip a wing or tail in hopes of damaging as many of them as possible. Finally, the remnants of the Japanese squadron fled in another direction.

Butch O'Hare made it back to the carrier where he reported the event. The film from the camera mounted on his plane showed the extent of his attempt to protect his fleet. He had, in fact, destroyed five enemy aircraft.

For his actions, Butch became the Navy's first flying ace of WWII and the first Naval aviator to win the Congressional Medal of Honor. A year later, Butch was killed in aerial combat at the age of twenty-nine.

His hometown would not allow the memory of this WWII hero to fade, and today, O'Hare Airport in Chicago is named in tribute to the courage of this great man.

So what do these two stories have to do with each other? Butch O'Hare was Easy Eddie's son.

What made a man like Eddie O'Hare decide to change? He decided what he wanted out of life. He wanted to leave a legacy for his son and a name Butch could be proud of. This became his true north, his *why*. Easy Eddie determined to live a life of virtue. Because of his choice, his son was able to inspire a nation.

It is important to think about living by virtue. It is more important to live by virtue. The Stoic philosophy is not a philosophy of ideas but one of action. All perception, attitudes and actions should be done in accordance with accomplishing these four virtues.

These virtues went on to be used by the Stoic theologians Ambrose, Augustine and Thomas Aquinas to describe the basis for the behavior and virtues of a Christian. They have become known to many as the cardinal virtues. These virtues did not originate with church fathers, they began with philosophers.

> *"You must have these principles at hand both night and day; you must write them down; you must read them."* [35]
>
> **// Marcus Aurelius**

Today, we would call these core values. You may have heard that term before. Your business probably has core values. Oftentimes, these are sentiments that look nice on a wall but don't change much about the way we act.

Enron was one of the largest energy companies in America with over $100 billion in revenues. They claimed to have a core value of integrity. They went bankrupt because of an SEC investigation that revealed wide-scale corporate fraud and corruption.

Core values don't matter when they're written. They matter when they are lived.

A life of virtue requires us to live by virtue. The only way to make sure that your life is good, that your perceptions, attitudes and actions are right, is to aim them at your virtues.

You don't have to choose the Stoic virtues as your own, but choose your virtues and live by them. Once you resolve to live by your virtues, nothing can stop you from succeeding. Because nothing can ever impede your ability, choose to practice your virtues. Your perceptions, attitudes and actions can line up with your virtues at any time and in any situation, regardless of what lies outside of your control. According to the Stoics, the only way to become a failure, the only way to live a bad life, is to fail to live by your virtues. The road to a good life begins and ends with living according to your virtues.

All of us need a cause. What cause could be more noble and just than to seek to live a life of virtue?

What virtues do you wish to live for?

14 // THE CONTROLLABLES

"There is only one way to happiness and that is to cease worrying about things that are beyond the power of our will." //**Epictetus**

Two traveling monks reached a town where there was a wealthy young woman waiting to step out of her sedan chair. Rain had made deep puddles, and she couldn't step across without spoiling her silken robes. She stood there, looking cross and impatient. She was scolding her attendants. They had nowhere to place the packages they held for her, so they couldn't help her across the puddle. She saw the monks and demanded that one of them help her cross the puddles.

The younger monk looked at the woman, said nothing, and walked by. The older monk quickly picked her up and put her on his back, transported her across the water, and put her down on the other side. She didn't thank the older monk, she just shoved him out of the way and departed.

As they continued on their way, the young monk was brooding and preoccupied. After several minutes, unable to hold his silence, he spoke out. "That woman back there was selfish and rude, but you picked her up on your back and carried her! Then she didn't even thank you!"

"I set the woman down hours ago," the older monk replied. "Why are you still carrying her?"

On Sept. 9, 1965, Commander James Stockdale was flying a mission to bomb a bridge in North Vietnam, skirting the treetops at 500 knots, when anti-aircraft flak brought his A-4 Skyhawk jet down.[36] He spent about thirty seconds floating under his parachute, realizing that he had broken bones in his left shoulder and back during his ejection. His next realization was that he was going to land in the middle of a village and be captured. "Five years down there, at least," he told himself. Upon landing, he was ripped from his parachute by the North Vietnamese and beaten severely.

They sat him up in the street; he looked around and noticed his left leg. "Broken at the knee and sticking out at a right angle toward nine o'clock. Crippled for life! I knew it in an instant. What a letdown," he later said.

Stockdale was taken to the POW camp in Hanoi—famously called the "Hanoi Hilton"—known for its brutality.

"You see, between the time I pulled the ejection handle and came to rest in that main street, I had become a man with a mission...I knew the whole setup—that the North Vietnamese already held about twenty-five prisoners, probably in Hanoi and, that as the only wing commander to survive an ejection, I would be their senior—their commanding officer—and would remain so, very likely, throughout this war that I felt sure would last at least another five years. And here I was starting off crippled and flat on my back...I took command (clandestinely, of course—the North Vietnamese would never acknowledge our rank) of about fifty Americans. That expatriate colony would grow to more than 450—all officers, all pilots or NFOs (Naval Flight Officer). I was determined to play well the given part." [37]

From the start, Commander Stockdale refused to cooperate with his captors. He rallied the troops around him using a system of wall taps, finger and toe signals, and hidden notes to communicate, creating a code of conduct that not only allowed them to survive their torturers but defy them.

When told by his captors that he was to be paraded in public, Stockdale slit his scalp with a razor to purposely disfigure himself so that his captors could not use him as propaganda. When they covered his head with a hat, he beat himself with a stool until his face was swollen beyond recognition. During his captivity, due to torture, his leg was broken twice.

When Stockdale was discovered with information that could implicate those around him, he broke a window in a torture room and slashed his wrist with the glass shards to show he'd die before telling the North Vietnamese anything. This act was credited with helping end the North Vietnamese use of excessive torture toward POWs. After this instance, Stockdale was isolated for a long period of time. One of his friends, David Hatcher was able to pass him a note written with rat droppings on toilet paper. It contained the last stanza of the poem *Invictus* by **William Ernest Henley**.[38]

Out of the night that covers me
Black as the pit from pole to pole,
I thank whatever gods may be
For my unconquerable soul.

In the fell clutch of circumstance,
I have not winced nor cried aloud.
Under the bludgeonings of chance
My head is bloody, but unbowed.

Beyond this place of wrath and tears
Looms but the Horror of the shade,

And yet the menace of the years
Finds, and shall find, me unafraid.

It matters not how strait the gate,
How charged with punishments the scroll,
I am the master of my fate:
I am the captain of my soul.

After being caught urging other POWs to resist, he and ten other senior POWs were taken to another jail block where they were frequently tortured. He led the POWs' culture of defiance, continuing to communicate with those under his command in such a way that gave them hope.

"We had a war to fight and were committed to fighting it from lonely concrete boxes," Stockdale said during a later interview. "Our very fiber and sinew were the only weapons at our disposal. Each man's values from his own private sources provided the strength enabling him to maintain his sense of purpose and dedication. They placed unity above self. Self-indulgence was a luxury that could not be afforded." [39]

James Stockdale was not a preacher. He didn't try to teach his men how to survive or tell them what to think. He didn't lecture them on high-minded ideals. He inspired them through the way he lived every day.

Stockdale was released eight years after his capture in February of 1973. For his actions in the POW camps, he was awarded the Medal of Honor on March 4, 1976.

In his book, *Good to Great*, **Jim Collins** recounts a conversation he had with Stockdale regarding his perspective during his period as a POW.

"I never lost faith in the end of the story, I never doubted not only that I would get out, but also that I would prevail in the end and turn the experience into the defining event of my life, which, in retrospect, I would not trade." [40]

What gave James Stockdale this perspective? During his time in the Navy, Stockdale had attended classes on philosophy at Stanford. He discovered the philosophy of the Stoics, in particular Epictetus, a slave who became a philosopher.

In the *Enchiridion*, Epictetus asserts that we should always strive to make the distinction between what is "up to us" and what is "not up to us." TA EΦ HMIN (Ta eph'hemin) - What is up to us. TA OYK EΦ HMIN (Ta ouk eph'hemin) - what is not up to us.

We all fundamentally know this to be true. We have discussed it here. There are some things that are up to us and some things that are not. It's simple. But simple ≠ easy.

What could Commander James Stockdale control? He couldn't control his physical pain; he couldn't determine when and if he was liberated. He couldn't control the cards that were dealt to him by life, the part he was assigned to play. But he could control himself. His thoughts, his attitudes and his actions.

"You have power over your mind – not outside events. Realize this, and you will find strength." [41]   **//Marcus Aurelius**

"Sickness is a hindrance to the body, but not to your ability to choose, unless that is your choice. Lameness is a hindrance to the leg, but

not to your ability to choose. Say this to yourself with regard to everything that happens, then you will see such obstacles as hindrances to something else, but not to yourself." [42] **// Epictetus**

We can only be held back if we wish to be. This is what James Stockdale knew. More than knowledge, this is what he lived for during the eight years as a prisoner of war.

What causes you the most worry and anxiety? If you are anything like me, it is those things that lie outside of your control. We hope and pray and wish that those things will work out for us. In all our hoping, praying and wishing, sometimes we can delude ourselves into believing that we can control the uncontrollable. That is impossible.

In 480 BC, Xerxes and 2.5 million soldiers from the Persian Empire invaded Greece. At one point, they came to a waterway called the Hellespont that separated Asia and Europe. The waters surged and destroyed the bridges that his engineers spent days building. In response, Xerxes beheaded the engineers and ordered that the river be given three hundred lashes and branded with hot irons. As the punishment was being delivered to the river, Xerxes' men were ordered to yell at the river, "you salt and bitter stream, your master lays this punishment upon you for injuring him, who never injured you."

Shortly before this, Xerxes had written a letter to a nearby mountain through which he was attempting to cut a canal. "You may be tall and proud," he wrote, "but don't you dare cause me any trouble. Otherwise, I'll topple you into the sea." [43]

If we're honest with ourselves, we must admit that we cannot predict and control most events we experience. Our attempts to be the master of the universe will at best make us anxious. At worst, like Xerxes we appear arrogant, petulant and insane: threatening mountains and spanking rivers as punishment. We may not be able to choose how the river flows, or the size of the mountain we face, but we can choose how we respond to it.

When **James Stockdale** was asked by Jim Collins who didn't make it out of Vietnam, he replied: *"Oh, that's easy, the optimists. Oh, they were the ones who said, 'We're going to be out by Christmas.' And Christmas would come, and Christmas would go. Then they'd say, 'We're going to be out by Easter.' And Easter would come, and Easter would go. And then Thanksgiving, and then it would be Christmas again. And they died of a broken heart. This is a very important lesson. You must never confuse faith that you will prevail in the end—which you can never afford to lose—with the discipline to confront the most brutal facts of your current reality, whatever they might be."* [44]

Jim Collins calls this the Stockdale paradox. We can't live in the future. We can only live in the now. Today is all we are given. This present moment is the only one we can exist in. There are good things about today and bad things about today. We cannot ever allow our hopes for the future to prevent us from facing the reality of our life today. We cannot allow the regrets of the past determine our actions right now.

Today, right now, you have this moment. You have this day. How will you control what you can control to ensure that you live by virtue?

After all, isn't that the goal? Not to seek happiness, safety or comfort but to be courageous when we are confronted by the reality of what we can't control.

"Our actions may be impeded ... but there can be no impeding our intentions or our dispositions. Because we can accommodate and adapt. The mind adapts and converts to its own purposes the obstacle to our acting. The impediment to action advances action. What stands in the way becomes the way." [45]   **// Marcus Aurelius**

Embracing the reality of what you can't control by controlling what you can is your only hope. It is your only way forward. There is no other way.

How much time do we spend saying, "None of this is my fault"? Admitting that so much in life lies outside our control? We are often professional blamers. We can make a great case to other people that none of our issues are our fault. After all, who could have blamed James Stockdale if he gave his captors some information to avoid pain? Many before him and after him were willing to give their enemies information to avoid torture.

We can convince ourselves that we cannot be blamed for what we face. Our upbringing, our culture, our mistreatment at the hands of others has made us this way.

By doing this, are our problems now solved? Determining blame doesn't stop the situation from happening.

"And why should we feel anger at the world? As if the world would notice!" [46] **// Marcus Aurelius**

The things you and I experience do not care about our feelings about them. The things we experience that are outside our control are not affected by our complaints, protestations or lamentations. The only way to overcome what you can't control is to control what you can.

Your thoughts, your attitudes and your actions. When you do this, you will find all that you need. Worry about whose fault it is later.

All good things (and bad things) must come to an end. The things that lie outside our control will always be outside of our control. Those things will come and go. Situations and circumstances will change, but we can remain steadfast in our thinking, attitudes and actions. And as the storms rage around us, we build what Marcus Aurelius calls our "inner citadel." An unchanging, internal and impenetrable fortress that guides our life.

Reinhold Niebuhr is credited with writing the *Serenity Prayer*:

> *God grant me the serenity to accept the things I cannot change, courage to change the things I can, and wisdom to know the difference.*

This is the prayer of the practicing Stoic.

15 // THE WORD

The idea of what is controllable and uncontrollable seem universal to us. The notion of thoughts, attitudes and actions make sense at a profound level. But where do these concepts come from? The things that seem to be universally true must emanate from somewhere. Also, who gets to determine what is good and bad? Who decides what is a virtue and what is a vice?

The Stoics believed that there was a fundamental universal principle called the logos (λόγος). The Greek word for reason, logos is where we get the word "logic." Logos represents the idea that the entire universe was governed by reason and rational thought.

This is what binds all of creation together. Tertullian referred to all matter as honey, and the logos was the honeycomb that binds it all together and gives it meaning. [47]

Heraclitus believed that the logos is eternal,[48] yet many of us have not heard of it. He asserted that those of us who have heard of it do not understand it. Through the logos, all things come into being, yet we cannot understand how logos works.

Life is a series of dots. To the Stoics, the logos was the thing that would make all these dots connect and become meaningful. Because of the logos, human beings can observe and rationally process the world we live in. We can then use our observations and experiences to create and form meaning for our own lives.

In Stoicism, the logos represented ultimate perfection. Although there is much that lies outside of our control, the logos controlled the uncontrollable. Human beings can focus on what they can control, because the providence of the logos guarantees that all that can't be controlled is part of the plan. The logos created the concept of virtue—core values—and when we decide to live by virtue, we are living according to the plan of the logos.

Because of the logos, whatever happens to us and around us that lies outside our control is destined to happen. But these events aren't bad, they are meant for our good. Therefore, no matter what happens to us, we can be happy, because the divine plan is greater than our perspective. And the part we play in the plan is to live by virtue.

"Do not seek for things to happen the way you want them to; rather, wish that what happens happen the way it happens: then you will be happy." [49] // **Epictetus**

""Accept the things to which fate binds you, and love the people with whom fate brings you together, but do so with all your heart." [50]

// **Marcus Aurelius**

The Stoics had a term for this "acceptance of fate": *amor fati*. The love of fate. We should not just accept what happens to us but love it, because it is part of the plan for our lives.

"My formula for greatness in a human being is amor fati: that one wants nothing to be different, not forward, not backward, not in all eternity. Not merely bear what is necessary, still less conceal it—all idealism is mendacity in the face of what is necessary—but love it." [51]

// **Nietzsche**

What we experience is not undesirable to the Stoics. In fact, it is preferred. Everything happens for a purpose, but that purpose is up to us to decide. One of the chief goals of life, according to modern Stoic and author **Robert Greene**, is to *"stop wishing for something else to happen, for a different fate. That is to live a false life."* [52]

Early Christians used to write "DV" or "Deo Volente" (God willing) at the end of letters. The Stoics referred to this as the reserve clause.

We live our lives and make our plans. We should always remember that our success is not guaranteed. Life is a vapor; we are always subject to the plans of God. We should live life and make our plan with the reserve clause in mind. That these things only will happen if God wills. Much of what happens to us will not be in accordance with our plan but God's plan. So we must amor fati—love what happens to us that lies outside of our control.

The book of James mentions this as well.

Look here, you who say, "Today or tomorrow we are going to a certain town and will stay there a year. We will do business there and make a profit." How do you know what your life will be like tomorrow? Your life is like the morning fog—it's here a little while, then it's gone. What you ought to say is, "If the Lord wants us to, we will live and do this or that."

// James 4:13-15

The goal is not just to be okay with what happens, or even feel good about it. The goal is to love it. Because if something happens to us outside of our control, it was meant to happen, and therefore, we are meant to make the best of it.

"The best-laid plans of mice and men often go awry." [53]

// Robert Burns

How often do we go through something that seems awful in a moment and then later see that it was better for us to experience that? Most often, we can only decide something is better in hindsight, after the story is written. What the Stoics believe is that we can be grateful for what happens to us in advance because of two things. First, it was inevitable; we could not have avoided it. If we could have avoided it, we would have. Second, because of the logos, it is meant for our good. So we can be grateful for all events that we encounter, good and bad, because it's a part of the plan. And the plan of the logos is always good.

No matter what we experience, good and bad, we should make every effort to carefully consider how we are responding. Without denying the reality of our experience, we must discover the meaning in those events that makes our life mean something. We decide what those moments mean. If our response to outside events is virtuous, we are well on our way to living a good life.

"If your impulse is without a 'reserve clause,' failure at once becomes an evil to you as a rational creature. But once you accept that universal necessity, you cannot suffer harm nor even be thwarted."

// Marcus Aurelius

DOT III // THE ROLE

16 // THE NEW BEGINNING

After four hundred years of silence, God started speaking again. The New Testament begins with four books that tell the same story. Matthew, Mark, Luke, and John. But these aren't just books. They are called Gospels. According to scholars, the word gospel is likely a combination of two Anglo-Saxon words that mean "to tell something good." The word is widely accepted to simply mean "good news."

These four books share the same basic outline, but they were written by different people. All of them were written around the same time and describe the career of Jesus and his ideas about life.

In the beginning the Word [logos (λόγος)] already existed. The Word [λόγος] was with God, and the Word [λόγος] was God. He existed in the beginning with God. God created everything through him, and nothing was created except through him. The Word [λόγος] gave life to everything that was created, and his life brought light to everyone. The light shines in the darkness, and the darkness can never extinguish it.

// John 1:1-5

The Gospel of John starts with a direct connection to Stoicism. To the Stoics, the logos was unknowable. It was the ethereal logic that governed our world. John starts by saying that the logos is not just knowable, it took the form of a person.

The New Testament world looks much different from what we see in the Old Testament. The nation of Israel, Abraham's family, is now occupied by the Roman Empire. For many years, they have been in one form of captivity or another, and Roman occupation is just another one in a long history.

The Old Testament speaks of a king who would one day return to restore the family of Abraham and set them free from their captivity once and for all. The Jews were anxiously waiting for the day when the Messiah—the Christ, a political revolutionary—would rise and restore their fortunes.

The story of Jesus is not one that starts out in greatness. We hear the story every Christmas. There's no room in the inn. He's born and placed in an animal feeding trough. His mother was a teenager who claimed that she was impregnated by an angel. His hometown is a small town in the middle of nowhere.

Much has been written and discussed about the life and message of Jesus. But the only records of his life are contained in the four Gospels. Virtually all modern scholars agree that he was a real person that lived, preached, was arrested by the Jewish authorities, and was crucified on the order of Pontius Pilate.

Most other things about the life of Jesus have been debated for centuries. Secular and religious scholars have countless interpretations and opinions on his life. Even within Christianity, there are major disagreements related to him.

James Allan Francis puts it this way in his essay, *One Solitary Life* [54]:

> *Here is a man who was born in an obscure village, the child of a peasant woman. He grew up in another village. He worked in a carpenter shop until He was thirty. Then for three years He was an itinerant preacher.*

"He never owned a home. He never wrote a book. He never held an office. He never had a family. He never went to college. He never put His foot inside a big city. He never traveled two hundred miles from the place He was born. He never did one of the things that usually accompany greatness. He had no credentials but Himself...

While still a young man, the tide of popular opinion turned against him. His friends ran away. One of them denied Him. He was turned over to His enemies. He went through the mockery of a trial. He was nailed upon a cross between two thieves. While He was dying His executioners gambled for the only piece of property He had on earth - His coat. When He was dead, He was laid in a borrowed grave through the pity of a friend.

Nineteen long centuries have come and gone, and today He is a centerpiece of the human race and leader of the column of progress.

I am far within the mark when I say that all the armies that ever marched, all the navies that were ever built; all the parliaments that ever sat and all the kings that ever reigned, put together, have not affected the life of man upon this earth as powerfully as has that one solitary life."

This essay reminds us of the significance of Jesus. Because of Jesus, we have a new covenant: the New Testament. Remember, the word testament? It means covenant. And if there's an Old Testament, there must be a new one.

The Old Testament is a covenant promise between God and the family of Abraham, and if you're not born into the family, you're out of luck.

Fortunately for us Gentiles, the New Testament changes the family dynamics. God says that anyone can now be part of Abraham's family if they want to. All it takes is our choice to be in the family.

A testament is still a covenant

The New Testament is still a covenant. There are still terms for both sides. In this new covenant, however, God also changes the terms. We're going to talk about the terms, but the Gospel of John starts by telling us that all of this is part of the plan. It's not part of the plan to let the family of Abraham keep the promise to themselves.

It is remarkable to me that John does this using logos, a word borrowed from philosophy. The word already had significant meaning before John ever used it. This was a philosophical word hundreds of years before its use in the book of John. John inextricably ties philosophy and theology forever: theology being the study of God and his nature, and philosophy being the human effort to decide how best to live.

John sets the foundation that we cannot have one without the other. A proper understanding of God requires us to understand ourselves. And a proper understanding of ourselves requires an understanding of God and his plan, the logos.

Jesus goes on to live a remarkable life. Even if we completely discount his divinity, he lives a life that we should aspire to imitate. His life, and therefore his philosophy, is marked by unselfishness, humility, forgiveness and fundamental love. And the bulk of the New Testament that follows the four Gospels is the attempt to contextualize his life and example into the human experience.

Regardless of your religious affiliation, there is much that can and should be gleaned from the life and example of Jesus in all our lives.

One of the inherent problems in the western world is that most people merely see Christianity as a belief system. Not a way of life. Many Christians can and have lived their whole life without studying the life of Jesus—a person they claim to follow. According to a Pew research study conducted in 2021, 63% of Americans claim to be Christian.[55]

In the western world, especially in America, being good and moral is what it means to be a Christian. In this same study, we see a decline in religious affiliation. More and more people see religion as unimportant. Along with other religions, people will always be changing religious affiliation. Religions are ways of believing. But there's a difference between believing something and living it out. Christianity has been relegated as one of the world's religions. If Christianity remains primarily a set of beliefs, it will become more and more irrelevant and impotent in the life of the average person. Jesus' goal in coming to the earth was not to give us a set of beliefs. His goal was to give us a new way to live. His goal was not to teach us to live moral lives. Jesus' goal was to teach us to live meaningful lives. Christianity is not meant to be just a religion; it is meant to be a way of life.

Those who have embraced this way of living have been responsible for some of the greatest achievements in history.

Eyeglasses were invented in the church.

The first Gregorian calendar was created by Catholic astronomers.

The science of genetics was founded in the church by an Augustinian friar named Gregor Mendel.

The theory of the big bang was first put forward by a Catholic priest, Georges Lemaitre.

The first ever universities and colleges started in churches beginning in the eleventh and twelfth centuries. To this day, 83 percent of the colleges in the US were founded through the church.

The first hospitals began in churches in the fourth century.

Some of the greatest art and artists in history happened because of the church. Raphael, Michelangelo, Da Vinci, Bernini and more were all supported by the church.

The first ever systematic bodies of law and law schools were founded in the church.

The Latin alphabet, the most widely used writing system in the world, was spread by the church.

There is overwhelming evidence that living like Jesus changes the world in practical, not just spiritual, ways. Changing the world doesn't happen because we believe in something; it happens because we live a certain way.

The word *"Christian"* was originally meant as an insult to early Christians. People would mock them by calling them *"little Christs."* Because of their desire to think, be, and do like they believed Jesus would. Can the same be said about Christians today?

Unfortunately, it seems that Christians have become known for what they oppose and despise. Christians have created a reputation that they care more about their viewpoint and agenda than they do about people. They have married themselves to political parties and ideologies as if these things were what Jesus lived and died for. The truth is, the only people Jesus is recorded being angry at were people who cared about their ideology and agenda more than people. Two thousand years ago, these people were called Pharisees. In many ways, we view them as the "bad guys" of the New Testament. Pharisees and modern-day Christians seem to have a lot in common.

The best philosophies aren't taught. The best philosophies are lived. The problem with many people who call themselves Christians is that they are bad at following Jesus. They are good at believing but fail miserably at living those beliefs out when it matters. Not because they don't understand the Bible enough—although that may be true—but because unlike the audience of the New Testament, most of us have little to no understanding of philosophy. Therefore, we place little emphasis on living out our beliefs. Even for those of us that call ourselves "Christian," Christianity is a set of beliefs we agree on, not a way that we live.

Jesus and the New Testament—*the new promise*—meant to establish a way of living, not just a way of believing. The life of Jesus was meant to show us how to live. Knowing and following Jesus represents the ultimate combination of theology and philosophy. We must know God, but we also must know ourselves and decide how we should live.

This is not merely a religion or a belief system to add to our perspective. This is a way of living that should change everything. This sounds simple, but simple ≠ easy.

Life is filled with gray areas. It's not as black and white as the words on this page. The world seems to be an evil place. And there are times that it only seems appropriate to live a life of "eye for an eye and tooth for a tooth." After all, that's in the Bible too.

Remember, you and I should only focus on what we can control. We cannot control the world or other people, only ourselves. We need to always remind ourselves of the tenets of our philosophy so we can stay focused on what we are supposed to be focused on.

There was a man who had a son that he loved very much. He would do his best to always make time for his son no matter how busy he was.

One night, as the father was working late in his office, his son came in to play with him. Wanting to finish his work, but also make time for his son, he looked around his office and saw a magazine. On the cover of the magazine was a large picture of the world. The father cut the cover off the magazine and tore the picture of the world into pieces. He called his son over to him and gave him the pile of torn paper from the cover of the magazine and went back to work.

The son ran out of his office and the man figured he had a few hours to get work done. Thirty minutes later, the boy burst into his father's office and said, "Okay, it's finished. Can we play now?"

"Let's go see," the father said not believing his son could have finished his task that quickly. Sure enough, there was the picture of the world, all put together, every piece in its place.

The father said, "That's amazing! How did you do that?"

"It was simple," the son said. "On the back of the page was a picture of a man. When I put the man together, the whole world fell into place."

Believe it or not, that's the goal of the New Testament. That's the goal of Jesus himself. You and I need to take our focus off the world and everyone else—all the things we can't control—and put the focus on ourselves. Understand what is up to us and do the best we can with what we have.

Let everyone else focus on what everyone else is doing, comparing themselves among themselves, deciding what behavior is appropriate based on what the people around them are doing. That's what they've always done. That's what got us into this mess and is keeping us there.

The world needs some people who have the ability, discipline and capacity to change themselves for the better so the world can change for the better too. There is hope because we don't have to do it alone. We don't have to figure it out by ourselves. There is a path that has been laid for us to follow.

You and I are a part of that plan. God put you on the earth for such a time as this. To be who we are right now. To understand that he has a plan, we are a part of that plan, and we can decide at any time to play a part.

17 // THE NEW PROMISE

Let's go back to who we started with: Abraham and his family. As we know, his family was in many ways deeply flawed. We'll never know the reason why God chose Abraham and his family. But one thing that they show us about God is that he doesn't wait for perfect people to make his plan happen. God is often simply looking for people who want to be part of the plan.

God promised that Abraham would have a son, and that his family would become a nation and that they would bless the world. But there was a problem. Abraham was old. Really old. It is believed he was around seventy-five when God made these promises to him. It wasn't until twenty-five years later that his son Isaac would be born. Twenty-five years is a long time. It's even longer when you're seventy-five.

Even though God made Abraham some promises, Abraham was human, like us. He didn't know how things were going to work out. What do we do when we don't know how things are going to work out? We worry. We focus on what we can't control. Abraham didn't just worry, he tried to make the promise happen on his own. He had a son named Ishmael with one of his servants, Hagar, which led to all kinds of problems for his family.

Abraham had a decision to make. He had to decide whether he was going to believe in the covenant that God had made. To believe that God would hold up his end of the covenant. Genesis 15 tells about his decision.

And Abram believed the LORD, and the LORD counted him as righteous because of his faith.

// Genesis 15:6

To state it another way, Abraham was considered good and virtuous because he believed God's promise. He was righteous—in right standing with God—just because he believed. Would you say that you are righteous? Most of us would say no. We associate righteousness with good, virtuous, or even perfect behavior. What does it mean that Abraham was counted as righteous? That's an important question. Families have been divided and wars have been fought over that question.

As we read the story of Abraham's family in the Old Testament, the answer to that question becomes clear for them. As we open the New Testament, that answer can become clear for us.

In the Old Testament, Abraham was given the same rights and privileges with God as a person who was perfect. These were given to him because of his faith, not because Abraham was a good man. He was human and broken just like us. But because he chose to believe and act on that belief, he was chosen.

Two thousand years later, the apostle Paul made a connection between Abraham's act of faith and those seeking a right standing with God in the New Testament church.

And because of Abraham's faith, God counted him as righteous. And when God counted him as righteous, it wasn't just for Abraham's benefit. It was recorded for our benefit, too, assuring us that God will also count us as righteous if we believe in him, the one who raised Jesus our Lord from the dead.

// Romans 4:22-24

Paul is saying that we are given the same choice that Abraham had. A choice to have faith in God's plan and promise. If we make that choice, we are given the same gift. This gift is directly connected to the promise God gave to Abraham thousands of years ago.

This gives us a lot of hoops to jump through. Jesus, God, righteousness, and faith? The idea of God granting righteousness because of faith is not how it is supposed to work. Think about your relationships with people. To be righteous means to be in right standing, in other words, to have a good relationship. Good relationships with human beings don't happen because of faith. In a human context, right relationships require right behavior. It's not enough for our friends and family that we have faith in them, we must treat them right. Otherwise, we risk damaging those relationships. If you want to have a good relationship with your friends, spouse or coworkers, it requires a certain kind of behavior. Even the strongest relationships are not unconditional. I'm married, and if I continually cheat on my wife, she may forgive me, but that doesn't mean that we are in a "right relationship." Why? Because my behavior is not right. If I want to have right relationships with people around me, I must behave right.

God did not choose Abraham because he was the best human on the planet. God didn't make a promise to Abraham because Abraham did all the right things. Abraham believed in God. Because Abraham believed in God and his promise, Abraham was God's friend. He was unconditionally accepted. Nothing else mattered. Not his behavior, lifestyle or personality. That kind of unconditional acceptance does not exist in human relationships.

God tells us that the way for us to be his friend is to believe in him and his promise. Faith is not just the foundation of a good relationship with God, it is the only thing God asks out of us. It's the only thing that God asked out of Abraham. That doesn't mean we have to have faith in everything God says right now. We just have to have faith in one thing he says. Look at Abraham: in Genesis 12, God invites him to step beyond what he knows into the unknown and the uncomfortable. To get started, we just need to be willing to take a step out from what we know into something that may feel unknown or foreign to us. That's the beginning of faith. That's where God starts with us: with our willingness to step from what we know into the unknown.

What is faith?

Now we should answer this question: What is faith? If faith is what enabled Abraham, and the same thing can enable us, we ought to know what faith looks like and acts like.

Faith is not a religious concept. It is a human concept. It is arguably one of the most powerful tools that we have. A simple definition of faith is the ability to believe something and act on that belief. Faith has initiated everything from life-saving medical developments to genocide. Faith fuels good and evil every day in every segment of the population. Everything that has been done, for good or bad, was done because someone believed that it could and should be done. Every problem that has been solved was solved because someone believed and acted based on their belief.

Faith is our action based on our belief.

Belief is a part of faith, but faith is more than just belief. Belief can fuel our imagination and anticipation. It enables us to picture a future for ourselves and the people around us. But faith is the thing that causes us to act as if that future is going to happen. That's what Abraham was counted as righteous for.

Now faith is the assurance (title deed, confirmation) of things hoped for (divinely guaranteed), and the evidence of things not seen [the conviction of their reality—faith comprehends as fact what cannot be experienced by the physical senses].

// Hebrews 11:1 AMP

The amplified version gives us a simple picture. Faith comprehends as fact what cannot be experienced by the physical senses. Faith is our ability to act as if what God says is true and that it's going to happen. It's the title deed. Faith is our ability to control what we can and entrust everything we can't to God. Imagine getting a deed to a piece of property that you've never seen. You don't have to see the land to own it, but you must trust that the land is there before you see it. Hebrews 11 reminds us of the story of Abraham:

It was by faith that Abraham obeyed when God called him to leave home and go to another land that God would give him as his inheritance. He went without knowing where he was going.

// Hebrews 11:8

That doesn't mean faith is blind. We can't live in the future. We can only live in the present. Faith is behaving in the present as if the future you see is going to happen. Faith is making a bet, taking a risk based on what you believe can happen. Faith is trusting that potential can become possible. Faith requires us to make a conscious decision to act as if a "maybe" is going to become a "yes." The Old Testament asks Abraham and his family, "Can you believe in something beyond yourself?" The New Testament asks all of us to believe that the logos—the divine word, principles, plans and promises of God—has been at work in humanity since the beginning.

Trusting in words and plans

The first recorded act of God is creation. God's method of creation was speaking. In Genesis 1, God "speaks" ten times to create the world. In Genesis 12, God speaks to Abraham before he does anything else. The Hebrew word used here is *amar* (אמר) that means to say, speak, intend, command and promise. The word *amar* is used repeatedly by God to introduce his plan to people. When we speak, what do we speak? Words. The Greek word for word is logos. When we amar, logos comes out of our mouth. Most of the time, we see our speech (amar) as just words (logos). But what if we spoke as if what we said created the world we live in? That's how God speaks.

In the Old Testament, we see how the spoken words of God are filled with his plans. The logos is communicated through speech. This speech is not mere words. These are the words. The speech (amar) is also the promise that the plan (logos) is going to come to pass. They are both the plan of God and the promise that the plan is going to happen.

You are created in God's image, so be careful about what you say—your amar. The words God says create the future. The words we say do the same. Death and life are in the power of amar. God's amar became the logos. What he said became the plan. What you say about your life right now creates the future of your life. What do you say about yourself? Your job? Your spouse? Your kids?

> *"So the Word [λόγος] became human and made his home among us. He was full of unfailing love and faithfulness. And we have seen his glory, the glory of the Father's one and only Son."*
> **// John 1:14**

The logos became evident in the life of a person. The person of Jesus. Much more than his teachings or his miracles, his life represents a culmination of thousands of years of planning and orchestration on God's part. God started in Genesis by speaking his plan to the family of Abraham through amar. The Stoics introduced the word to the rest of us as logos. Then Jesus tied everything together. Jesus is the plan (*logos*) and the spoken promises attached to it (*amar*).

Paul echoes this in Colossians:

Christ is the visible image of the invisible God. He existed before anything was created and is supreme over all creation, for through him God created everything in the heavenly realms and on earth. He made the things we can see and the things we can't see—such as thrones, kingdoms, rulers, and authorities in the unseen world. Everything was created through him and for him. He existed before anything else, and he holds all creation together.

// Colossians 1:15-17

Jesus is the honeycomb of Tertullian. He is the plan, promise and commands of God that became a person. He is the logos and the amar. His life itself is the plan we are meant to follow. The Stoics believed that virtue was defined by the logos. The life of Jesus shows us what it means to live a virtuous life. Virtue isn't self-defined. Nor is it defined by an unknowable entity. Virtue is defined by God himself in Scripture and displayed in the way Jesus lived.

God is asking us to trust and follow his plan, and that plan is a person. Trust and belief are different. We start the journey by believing that God has a plan, believing that he wants to use us. But we must arrive at the point where we trust in him and live life the way Jesus did. Faith and virtue.

If we read the book of Acts, chapter 17, it gives us even more context. It tells us that the apostle Paul spent time debating and getting to know Stoic philosophers in Athens (as well as Epicureans). He tried to teach them that the conclusion of their search was not the unknown logos, but Jesus himself. The purpose of their searching and seeking through philosophy was ultimately for them to find God.

The same was true for the Jews. The plan, promise, intention and spoken word of God became a person.

> *"His [God's] purpose was for the nations to seek after God and per-haps feel their way toward him and find him—though he is not far from any one of us. For in him we live and move and exist. As some of your own poets have said, "We are his offspring."*
>
> **// Acts 17:27-28**

Some of what you know and have heard about Jesus can be hard to believe, and therefore hard to trust. God is not asking for blind faith. Christians don't believe in the miracles of Jesus and the plan of God just because the "Bible says so." They believe because Matthew, Mark, John, Peter and James were eyewitnesses that said so. They saw it happen.

Luke, a first-century doctor, claimed to have thoroughly investigated the events surrounding the life and death of Jesus and concluded that Jesus was much more than just a moral man. He spent the second half of his life traveling through the Roman Empire telling that story. We believe because Paul believed. Paul, who was a persecutor and tormentor of Christians, came to believe that Jesus was the fulfillment of the Jewish law, the logos itself, the Son of God and that he physically rose from the dead. Christians believe because those who came after these men also came to believe and trust. From Clement, Ignatius, and Polycarp. To Justin Martyr, Origen, Tertullian, Ambrose, and Augustine. Thomas Aquinas, John Wycliffe,

Martin Luther, and Søren Kierkegaard all the way through the Great Awakenings in America and today.

Thousands, maybe millions of people from all walks of life have paid a high price—many have been martyred—because of their faith in Jesus. This is not blind faith; this is not being caught up in feelings. This is reason, belief and trust.

Being part of the promise requires faith. Specifically, faith in a person, Jesus. Not just belief, but the ability and courage to act based on that belief.

18 // THE RELATIONSHIP

If you were raised in a religious home, or attended a religious school, it was probably the rules that made you question whether that religion had a place in your future. Rules can make us feel judged and ostracized. And rules often aren't evenly applied, so religion also seems to breed endless hypocrisy.

Many religious people believe in their religion, but don't live what they believe. In other words, they are bad philosophers: bad at living out their values. Good at believing, bad at behaving.

Religious people love loopholes. They look for loopholes in their faith systems to avoid more restrictive rules. Many Catholics have found ways to justify birth control. Only a percentage of Muslims pray with their faces to the ground five times a day. Just a small number of Christians show the type of kindness, love, and forgiveness that Jesus modeled. Every major faith tradition teaches some form of the Golden Rule: Do unto others as you would have them do unto you. But we're all guilty of excusing our way around that rule. Bad news, we're all hypocrites, not just religious people.

Despite that, all faith systems agree that to be in good standing, followers need to keep the rules. Belief and behavior are central to every major religion in the world. Obedience determines whether you are a good Muslim, Christian, or Jew. Whether it's the Five Pillars of Islam, the Ten Commandments of ancient Judaism, or Jesus' Sermon on the Mount, rules define proper and improper behavior within a system.

We also live in a world that rewards performance. It's ingrained in us from an early age. Answer the test questions right and you pass. Answer wrong and you fail. Score the most points and win. Score one point less than the other team and you lose. Do well in school and you'll get a good job. Do well at work and you'll get a promotion. In the world we live in, performance matters.

Just about every aspect of life works that way. So why wouldn't it be the same way with God? If God created the world, wouldn't he want us to perform for him? Shouldn't our relationship with him be based on our ability to follow his rules? Isn't there a relationship between our ability to follow rules and perform for God and his happiness with us?

Our culture's focus on performance has the potential to shape our assumptions about God and Jesus. Answer these questions:

What do you have to do to make God happy?

What do you have to do to keep God happy?

We know there are always exceptions to rules. A student fails an exam by two points, and a professor finds a way to give them a passing grade. A sales associate makes a less-than-stellar presentation, loses an account, and their manager responds by giving them another chance. A driver is rear-ended and, upon discovering the challenging circumstances of the careless driver, decides not to make an issue of it.

Sometimes we don't get what we deserve.

It's great not to suffer consequences for what we've done, but it also feels like we've cheated the system. Shouldn't people get what they deserve? Isn't that fair? Isn't that just?

Making a deal with God

Have you ever tried to make a deal with God? Like Charles Barkley in *Space Jam*? ("Please give me my basketball powers back! I promise I'll never swear again. I'll never get another technical. I'll never trash-talk. I'll never go out with Madonna again.")

Bargaining is based on two assumptions. First, someone has something that we want or need. Second, that person isn't going to be easily convinced to help us. Most religious systems foster this mentality, and understandably so. That's how the world works. We often look at God as if he is not going to do anything for us unless we make him happy. He could love us, but we have to negotiate with him to get him to see that we are worthy of his love. We think God will not allow us to have a good life, meaningful existence, or success unless we follow all the right rules. We live as if we need to prove to God that we are worthy of his love, acceptance and blessing. We're trying to make God happy, and if we think he's happy, we're trying to keep him happy so that he won't hurt us.

God created us. He knows us. Everything about us. He knows things about us that we don't know about ourselves. He's not asking us to bargain with him, convince him to love us or believe in us. He's asking us to be like Abraham. Remember what Paul said?

"And because of Abraham's faith, God counted him as righteous."
// Romans 4:22

Is feeling good the same as being good?

Abraham was righteous because of his faith. Let's revisit righteousness.

If we're not careful, we can start to confuse our own righteousness with God's righteousness.

In other words, we can start to confuse feeling like we're in right standing with actually being in right standing. If we have a good day and feel like we mostly followed the rules and performed well that day, we can feel righteous. If we have a bad day and feel like we mostly ignored the rules, we can feel unrighteous. This feeling of "goodness" based on how well we do something is called self-righteousness. Self-righteousness is different from morality. Self-righteousness is how good you feel when you do "good" things, and how bad you feel when you do "bad" things. Guilt, self-righteousness and bargaining are often tied together. When we don't feel righteous, we feel guilty. Because we feel guilty, we attempt to bargain with God so we can feel righteous again.

We want to believe that our attempts to be good somehow make us righteous. We may sound a lot like **Abraham Lincoln**, who said, *"When I do good I feel good, when I do bad I feel bad, and that's my religion."* [56]

The book of Isaiah says this about self-righteousness:

> *"We are all infected and impure with sin. When we display our righteous deeds, they are nothing but filthy rags. Like autumn leaves, we wither and fall, and our sins sweep us away like the wind."*
>
> **// Isaiah 64:6**

In the ancient world, when women would menstruate, they would use old rags and then dispose of them. This is the term used here to denote "filthy rags." God says that our attempts at righteousness, doing good deeds, and performance matter to him as much as those rags would matter to us. Sin is something that infects us, and no amount of good we do can cover it up or hide it. No matter how hard we try, we can't do enough good to have a good relationship with God on our own. Does that mean good behavior doesn't matter? Of course, good behavior matters. But does good behavior make us right with God? Nope. It never will. Good behavior may be the thing that makes our relationship with people work, but it's not the thing that makes our relationship with God work. We can work our whole life to be "good enough" for God, and we still won't. God doesn't ask us to be good enough, he asks us to have faith. That's it. The starting point with God is not good behavior, it's faith.

If faith is action based on belief, then our behaviors should become better as our belief in God increases.

This may seem like I am contradicting myself. I've talked about poor philosophers a few times. Let me ask you some more questions.

What does God need from you?

What do people need from you?

God needs your faith. People need you to be good. We must live good lives because our lives affect the people around us. God knows you. He created you. He is with you on your worst day. He's not going to start loving you because you act good. He's not going to stop loving you because you act bad. If you've read the Old Testament, you've probably noticed a pattern—the creative and constant ways by which humanity fails. And the faithfulness of God to help us figure out a way back onto the right path. We should try to be good, but our goodness by itself will still result in our failure. That's why we need to start by simply having faith in God.

In Christianity, the perpetual failure we experience has become known as sin. Some of us, me included, don't like this word all that much. It seems judgmental and antiquated. So, we often will say that we make mistakes. We know that we aren't perfect and often fall short. But to be a "sinner" can feel harsh to us. If someone called me a sinner today, I'd probably become offended and defensive. So, I prefer to say that I make mistakes.

A mistake is an action or judgment that is misguided or wrong. We consider mistakes to be accidental. What about mistakes that we make on purpose?

And what do you call the person who makes the same mistakes on purpose over and over? A mistaker?

Most of us feel like Paul.

> *"I have discovered this principle of life—that when I want to do what is right, I inevitably do what is wrong. I love God's law with all my heart. But there is another power within me that is at war with my mind. This power makes me a slave to the sin that is still within me. Oh, what a miserable person I am! Who will free me from this life that is dominated by sin and death?"*
>
> **// Romans 7:21-24**

Sin is a Greek word that comes from archery. In archery, to sin means to miss what you are aiming for. If we're aiming for the bullseye and we miss, we have sinned. We don't like to be called a sinner though because it makes us feel condemned and disqualified. But there's a tension because if we're honest with ourselves, we don't just make mistakes by accident. There are a lot of mistakes we make on purpose.

A sinner is any person who knows the difference between right and wrong and chooses wrong. If we listen to the average street preacher, not only does being a sinner mean we're going to hell, it also means that God is looking forward to seeing us there.

What should we do? Most of us just try harder. And like Paul, we discover that the harder we try, the further we seem to fall. This isn't a new principle. This has been happening since the very beginning. All the way back to Adam, Eve, Abraham, Isaac and Jacob.

Many people run away from this entire proposition and see God as either nonexistent or evil and capricious, saying something like the Richard Dawkins quote mentioned in Part I. We often feel that we don't understand why God would create us this way and then punish us for being the way we are. And no matter how far we run, or how angry we get, we still struggle with what Isaiah 64 calls the "infection" of sin: the infection of making mistakes on purpose.

There are really only two responses to sin. Trying harder or realizing we do not have the ability to hit the target and asking for help.

When Jesus talked about sin, he made it so inclusive that nobody could escape the label. He said things like:

> *"You have heard the commandment that says, 'You must not commit adultery.' But I say, anyone who even looks at a woman with lust has already committed adultery with her in his heart."*
> **// Matthew 5:27-28**

The standard is so high, the target so far away. None of us can hit it. Paul says in Romans 3 that we are all sinners. We all constantly and consistently miss the mark. We know this to be true. This is part of being human. And most of us live hoping that the good one day will outweigh the bad. If we try harder, we can hit the target someday. Do better tomorrow. Or not. There's always next week.

Hitting the bullseye some of the time, every time

Sin has been around as long as humans have. In the first century, John the Baptist showed up in the region of Judea preaching and baptizing. In addition to the Gospels, John the Baptist is referenced in the Koran as well as by the Jewish historian Jocephus. John's message was harsh, but thousands of people flocked to the Jordan River to hear him. One afternoon while baptizing people in the Jordan River, John looked up and saw Jesus standing in line, waiting his turn. In that moment, he was amazed, and connected that moment to something deeply significant to all of us, sin.

> *"The next day John saw Jesus coming toward him and said, 'Look! The Lamb of God who takes away the sin of the world!'"*
>
> **// John 1:29**

In the Old Testament, God made some rules that governed the family of Abraham, the Israelites. One rule included a provision for how to handle when people sinned. When a person sinned, they were required to sacrifice an animal to God, usually a pure and spotless lamb. The animal's blood would atone for, or cover, the sin committed. This was a visceral reminder of the cost of sin and the need for forgiveness from God. No one believed that the blood of an animal was equal to the blood of a human being. But according to the old covenant, the blood of an animal was enough. The challenge was that the sacrifices had to be offered continually and repeatedly. There was no final or ultimate sacrifice for sin. To this day, the Jewish people celebrate Yom Kippur, or the day of atonement, as a day set aside for repentance to God and others.

John's statement in the Jordan River was a game-changer. He was asserting that once and for all, Jesus would atone for all sins. Past, present and future, a final sacrifice to fulfill the covenant made between God and his people in the Old Testament. Now it wasn't just for the family of Abraham, it was for the entire world. He's not just the logos that the philosophers talk about, he's the final sacrifice that fulfills the old covenant. The culmination of 1,500 years of history.

Twenty or so years after Jesus' crucifixion, the apostle Paul described the significance of that event this way:

> *"You were dead because of your sins and because your sinful nature was not yet cut away. Then God made you alive with Christ, for he forgave all our sins. He canceled the record of the charges against us and took it away by nailing it to the cross."*
>
> **// Colossians 2:13-14**

Through Christ, God has canceled the effects of our sin—our inability to hit the target. When we place our faith in Jesus and decide to follow him, our sin is forgiven. God knows we can't hit the target, so he decided to do it for us. That's called grace.

> *"God saved you by his grace when you believed. And you can't take credit for this; it is a gift from God. Salvation is not a reward for the good things we have done, so none of us can boast about it."*
>
> **// Ephesians 2:8-9**

When we choose to have faith, we experience this gift of grace. It is impossible to act our way into this kind of relationship, and we don't have to perform to stay there. Once and for all, God did what we could not, and can never do: he hit the target.

Jesus took our sin—each one of us—and paid for it once and for all. It doesn't matter if we missed the mark because Jesus didn't. Grace and forgiveness are gifts, not something we earn, and it's not just for Abraham's family. It's for all of us. But like any gift, it must be received. God isn't asking us to feel self-righteous for him. He's not trying to bargain with us so we earn his forgiveness. God is trying to give us a gift; faith is the only way to accept this gift.

It's not about being a good person for God. It's not about accepting a belief system. It's about understanding that we are incapable of being good on our own. Philosophy by itself will help us be better humans. But being a better human will only get us so far. God wants us to know him. He created us, he loves us, and he wants us to realize that his eternal plan was to bring us all into his family just like he did with Abraham. It has taken thousands of years of human history to get to this point. That's how deep it goes. That's the logos at work.

Because of our faith—our action based on our belief—we are God's friend. Just like Abraham. Our right standing with God is a gift from him, and it's only through his grace and our faith that we experience this righteousness. God's grace is not something we earn, it's something he freely gives. This gift has never been and will never be based on our performance.

When we have faith and believe that Jesus is who he said he is, God extends us the grace that puts us in right standing with him.

Our faith + God's grace = Righteousness.

Performance or our ability to follow rules doesn't factor into that equation.

What about the rules? Why are they important?

Think back to a time when a person extended grace to you. Try to remember the most extreme case—an event where you received something so undeserved and unexpected that you weren't even sure you could accept it. Have you ever been embarrassed by the significance of a gift? Now imagine if the person who forgave you or gave you an unexpected gift said, "I don't want anything in return. This is a no-strings-attached gift. But if you feel the need to thank me, simply pay it forward to someone else in need." Most likely, you would look for opportunities to do just that.

That's how Jesus told his followers to live. That's the part we're supposed to play. That's why we must go beyond faith. We must determine to be good to others like God is good to us..

19 // THE RULE

In the Old Testament, God gives the Israelites the Ten Commandments.

1. Do not have any other Gods before Me.
2. Do not worship anything except Me.
3. Do not use My name in vain.
4. Remember the Sabbath day.
5. Honor your father and mother.
6. Do not murder.
7. Do not commit adultery.
8. Do not steal.
9. Do not lie.
10. Do not covet.

These Ten Commandments went on to form the basis of all Jewish law.

These are simple principles that govern personal ethics as well as a relationship to God. By the time Jesus showed up in the New Testament, 603 laws had been added to these original ten. It was a full-time job trying to learn, understand and apply these 613 laws to the Jewish community.

These were divided into positive (do this) and negative (don't do this) commandments.

There were 365 negative commands, one for each day of the year. And there were 248 positive commands, one for each bone and main organ in the human body as they understood it.

This list was also further divided in many ways depending on the scholar that was interpreting the law.

These commands varied from things like:
- ▲ Know that God exists (Exodus 20:2)
- ▲ Pray to God daily (Exodus 23:25)
- ▲ Don't take revenge or have grudges (Leviticus 19:18)

To
- ▲ Men can't wear women's clothes and vice versa (Deuteronomy 22:5)
- ▲ Don't sacrifice your children in a fire to idols (Leviticus 18:21)
- ▲ Don't eat the fruit of a tree its first three years (Leviticus 19:23)
- ▲ No magic allowed (Deuteronomy 18:10)
- ▲ Don't sacrifice animals bought with the wages of a prostitute, or any animal that you exchanged for a dog (Deuteronomy 23:19)

People that were experts in the law, like the religious experts, believed that obedience to the law was the way they related to and pleased God.

Then Jesus showed up in Israel and began teaching. He gained a following. He seemed to have a deep command of Jewish law. But if you ask the religious leaders of that time, he was not one of them. He was saying that other things were more important than the law, which didn't fit their narrative. They were always trying to test and catch Jesus, trying to show how much he didn't know. By doing this, they hoped to reveal him as a false teacher and turn his followers away.

In Luke 10, there is an exchange just like this.

One day an expert in religious law stood up to test Jesus by asking him this question: "Teacher, what should I do to inherit eternal life?" Jesus replied, "What does the law of Moses say? How do you read it?" The man answered, "You must love the Lord your God with all your heart, all your soul, all your strength, and all your mind. And, Love your neighbor as yourself." "Right!" Jesus told him. "Do this and you will live!" The man wanted to justify his actions, so he asked Jesus, "And who is my neighbor?"

// Luke 10:25-29

Who is my neighbor?

Jesus does something revolutionary here. He takes every law, all 613 of them, and he turns them into one. The New Testament calls this the Great Commandment.

Love God with everything you have and love your neighbor as yourself.

What's the response of this expert in religious law? He sought to justify his actions. Remember this, whenever we try to justify our actions, we are making an impossible argument. What we are trying to say is that we were controlled by the external. A situation or a person was a certain way, and that caused us to act in a certain way. This is never true. We are always in control of our perceptions, attitudes and actions. The expert knew this, so did Jesus. Jesus tells this story:

"A Jewish man was traveling from Jerusalem down to Jericho, and he was attacked by bandits. They stripped him of his clothes, beat him up, and left him half dead beside the road.

"By chance a priest came along. But when he saw the man lying

there, he crossed to the other side of the road and passed him by. A Temple assistant walked over and looked at him lying there, but he also passed by on the other side.

"Then a despised Samaritan came along, and when he saw the man, he felt compassion for him. Going over to him, the Samaritan soothed his wounds with olive oil and wine and bandaged them. Then he put the man on his own donkey and took him to an inn, where he took care of him. The next day he handed the innkeeper two silver coins, telling him, 'Take care of this man. If his bill runs higher than this, I'll pay you the next time I'm here.'

"Now which of these three would you say was a neighbor to the man who was attacked by bandits?" Jesus asked. The man replied, "The one who showed him mercy." Then Jesus said, "Yes, now go and do the same."

// Luke 10:30-37

The term *Good Samaritan* has been in our cultural vocabulary for a long time. But it is important that we understand the power of this story.

Back then, if Jews had any mortal enemy, it was the Samaritans. Samaritans had intermarried with pagan nations and were seen as unfaithful to the family of Abraham, and to God. They lived in their own community, and Jews were forbidden to associate with them. To Jews, Samaritans were inherently evil. In fact, the idea of a "good" Samaritan was an oxymoron to a Jew.

In their mind, Jews had every reason to disdain and reject Samaritans. The religious expert's question is an attempt to make that distinction, arguing that some people were neighbors and others were not. And their responsibility should only be to love God's people.

Is what we see in Christianity today a reflection of this? How do Christians act toward the Muslim community, or the LGBT+ community? Are they our neighbors? What about people you and I just don't like very much? What about the family members we only see at Thanksgiving and Christmas?

The difference between the Samaritan, priest and temple assistant in this story was not what they saw, it's what they did with what they saw. The priest and the temple assistant knew the law, so they knew they had every reason to justify their actions.

In other words, they were more concerned with who qualified as their neighbor than being a good neighbor.

But Jesus changed everything, he makes it clear that truly pleasing and relating to God is all about how we treat people. Jesus makes this even clearer:

> *"So if you are presenting a sacrifice at the altar in the Temple and you suddenly remember that someone has something against you, leave your sacrifice there at the altar. Go and be reconciled to that person. Then come and offer your sacrifice to God."*
>
> **// Matthew 5:23-24**

Last chapter we talked about sacrifice and atonement. Now that we understand those things, we can see this verse in a different light. One of the most important things that a Jew could do was to offer sacrifices at the temple. There was only one temple, and it was in Jerusalem. Jews would travel for days from across the country and wait for a long time to be able to offer a sacrifice. Jesus says that nothing—including the offering of sacrifices—is more important than having a right relationship with your neighbor.

In other words, who cares if you call yourself a "Christian"? Who cares if you feed the poor or give money or time to the less fortunate? The fundamental thing that matters is that you are in right relationship with everyone around you. That's true sacrifice. Instead of worrying about being right, worry about being in relationship. Give up your right to be right so that you can have a right relationship.

These words today are still a challenge for every person that reads them. Remember what Jesus said. The only thing that matters is to love God and love the people around you. In this story, the expert in religious law gets it, a neighbor is one who shows mercy to those who are hurting and in need of help.

"When you wake up in the morning, tell yourself: The people I deal with today will be meddling, ungrateful, arrogant, dishonest, jealous, and surly. They are like this because they can't tell good from evil." [57] **// Marcus Aurelius**

We all want to justify our actions. There are people we don't like, people who are wrong, people who bother us. But what should our response be to such people? We should always be ready to be a neighbor to them. To love them.

Marcus Aurelius tells us to be ready for them. Jesus tells us what to do once they show up in our life.

Paul goes on to echo this. Owe nothing to anyone—except for your obligation to love one another. If you love your neighbor, you will fulfill the requirements of God's law. For the commandments say, "You must not commit adultery. You must not murder. You must not steal. You must not covet." These—and other such commandments—are summed up in this one commandment: "Love your neighbor as

*yourself." Love does no wrong to others, so love fulfills the require-
ments of God's law.*

// Romans 13:8-10

Jesus takes 613 laws, and he condenses them into one simple law.
To be obedient to God's law is to love him and love each other. **But
simple ≠ easy.** We all have and will struggle with this.

One law to rule them all

*"The greatest single cause of atheism in the world today is Chris-
tians who acknowledge Jesus with their lips and walk out the door
and deny Him by their lifestyle. That is what an unbelieving world
simply finds unbelievable."* [58]   **// Brennan Manning**

The Old Testament is primarily centered around getting to know
God and understanding how to follow his rules. This became the primary focus for ancient Jews. The proof that they knew God was how
well they followed the rules. This was the old promise. The old law.

There's a new promise and a new law. God intended to bring this
one into the world all along. When you get a new car, you don't keep
driving your old one. When you get a new house, you don't continue
living in your old house. When we get a new promise, we don't keep
living by the old one. That doesn't mean the old one ceases to exist.
It means that living in the new promise and following Jesus fulfills
the requirements of the old promise. So instead of 613 rules, we
have one. And if we follow the one, it counts as if we followed all 613.

The Old Testament was for a chosen few. The New Testament is for
all of us. But it is meant to be applied individually and personally.
The only way to truly love people is to understand the love that has
been given, undeservedly to each one of us.

The golden rule tells us to do to others what we would like them to do to us. Jesus says that is the essence of everything in the Old Testament.

> *You have heard the law that says, "Love your neighbor" and hate your enemy. But I say, love your enemies! Pray for those who persecute you! In that way, you will be acting as true children of your Father in heaven. For he gives his sunlight to both the evil and the good, and he sends rain on the just and the unjust alike. If you love only those who love you, what reward is there for that? Even corrupt tax collectors do that much. If you are kind only to your friends, how are you different from anyone else? Even pagans do that. But you are to be perfect, even as your Father in heaven is perfect.*
>
> **// Matthew 5:43-48**

When Jesus tells his followers to be perfect. He doesn't mean to be perfect in lifestyle, he means to practice perfect love. Like he did, like he does.

1 Corinthians 13 tells us what kind of love this is. It speaks to us as plainly today as it did when Paul wrote these words.

> *If I could speak all the languages of Earth and of angels, but didn't love others, I would only be a noisy gong or a clanging cymbal. If I had the gift of prophecy, and if I understood all of God's secret plans and possessed all knowledge, and if I had such faith that I could move mountains, but didn't love others, I would be nothing. If I gave everything I have to the poor and even sacrificed my body, I could boast about it; but if I didn't love others, I would have gained nothing.*
>
> *Love is patient and kind. Love is not jealous or boastful or proud or rude. It does not demand its own way. It is not irritable, and it keeps no record of being wronged. It does not rejoice about in-*

justice but rejoices whenever the truth wins out. Love never gives up, never loses faith, is always hopeful, and endures through every circumstance.

Prophecy and speaking in unknown languages and special knowledge will become useless. But love will last forever! Now our knowledge is partial and incomplete, and even the gift of prophecy reveals only part of the whole picture! But when the time of perfection comes, these partial things will become useless.

When I was a child, I spoke and thought and reasoned as a child. But when I grew up, I put away childish things. Now we see things imperfectly, like puzzling reflections in a mirror, but then we will see everything with perfect clarity. All that I know now is partial and incomplete, but then I will know everything completely, just as God now knows me completely.

Three things will last forever—faith, hope, and love—and the greatest of these is love.

// 1 Corinthians 13:1-13

The word Paul uses here for love is the word agape (ἀγάπη). Much has been written on what agape love is. It is the highest form of love, a love that is unconditional and not circumstantial. A love that is based on who the lover is, not what the object of love happens to be. Love that is a part of the nature and the character of the lover. Love that is a virtue. Love that guides thoughts, attitudes and actions. Perfect love.

God is love. Jesus says that we should be too.

How can we know that we are loving? *If our thoughts are guided by love.*

What are your thoughts toward people? All people, including those you struggle with?

How can we know we are loving? *If our attitudes are guided by love.*

What are our feelings toward these same people?

How can we know we are loving? *If our actions are guided by love.*

What are our actions toward these people?

In the book of John, Jesus talks this way about love.
"This is my commandment: Love each other in the same way I have loved you." // **John 15:12**

How can we understand God's love? By getting to know him. How do we get to know him? Through the stories of people that know him. Through the Bible, the collection of old and new promises that show us his thoughts, attitudes and actions toward humanity.

Once we begin to understand the love of God. Then we can begin to understand ourselves in proper context. We can see that we have the power at any time to control what we can control and let go of the things we can't. Including the thoughts, attitudes and actions of other people. We can trust him to take care of everything that we can't control. Because we know he loves us.

Once we know God and ourselves, and how he loves us, then we can understand the part that we can play. Our part is to express his love to the world through how we decide to think, feel and act toward people. To be the Samaritan.

We must also be always ready to deal with people who have not taken this journey to understand what we now know. We will be faced with challenges, difficulties and the evils of this world. We cannot allow those things to dictate our response. Our responses to the failures, evils and difficulties we face should be rooted and grounded in how we know that God responded to us. Love.

Jesus tells us that's all there is now. That's all that matters.

Loving is hard when you have a big but

This is where modern Christianity has missed the boat. People care more about the belief system than the action. It is easy to believe something in your head and heart—but deeply difficult to live it out. After all, Christians are humans too.

What should we do with people who seem to be evil, abusive or criminal? Back in 1 Corinthians 13, there's an interesting statement that Paul makes, and it doesn't seem to be connected to love.

Now we see things imperfectly, like puzzling reflections in a mirror, but then we will see everything with perfect clarity. All that I know now is partial and incomplete, but then I will know everything completely, just as God now knows me completely.

// 1 Corinthians 13:12

Life is imperfect. There is so much gray area that we encounter daily. Unfair, or even unjust, things happen to us. How should we respond to these things?

It's hard to try to live these things out. What Paul is saying is that one day, we will see the big picture. If hindsight is 20/20, eternal hindsight is 20/10. One day, the entire picture of our whole life will be in focus, and everything will make sense. Today is not that day though. Today seems puzzling and unclear.

So, what we should do when we don't know what to do is err on the side of love. There's a lot of mistakes we can make. If we're going to make a mistake, our mistake should be to love people too much rather than not enough. Be too forgiving, too generous, too kind, and let the chips fall where they may.

Let everything that you can control be rooted and grounded in loving people like God loves them, and let him take care of everything else.

"When you don't know what to say or do, ask, what does love require of you?" [59] **// Andy Stanley**

Your response to this might be something like, "Yeah, I get that, but..." The problem with loving people is usually one of *ands* and *buts*.

Love my neighbor *and* make the decision about who my neighbors are and what they look like.

Love my neighbor *but* make sure I feel comfortable.

Love my neighbor *and* make sure that they share my political/social/economic agenda.

Love my neighbor *but* justify my actions.

Love my neighbor *and* be pro-(insert here).

Love my neighbor *but* only surround myself with people/voices that agree with me.

Love my neighbor *and* be entitled to my opinion of them.

Love my neighbor *but* be intolerant of the things about them I don't like.

Love my neighbor *but* prove them wrong.

Love my neighbor *and* prove myself right.

There are a lot of *ands* and *buts* we can have. If we decide to lay down these things, there are a lot of implications to our ideology, politics, prejudices and doctrines. But that's what Jesus was aiming for two thousand years ago, and that's what he's aiming at now.

20 // THE TRUTH

"Wait a second," you might say. "There is an *and* attached to love in the Bible. Truth." [a]

That is true. There is love and there is truth.

The concept of truth is extensive. The prevailing attitudes in culture would tell us that truth is subjective. Truth is a social construct; that is not at all what Jesus or Scripture represents. The concept of truth is settled.

John 1 tells us that Jesus came in grace and truth. In John 8, Jesus tells us that we will know the truth and the truth will set us free. In John 14, Jesus declares that he is the way, the truth and the life. Objective truth matters. Objective truth exists. And it exists in the life and person of Jesus.

Paul says it this way:

This will continue until we all come to such unity in our faith and knowledge of God's Son that we will be mature in the Lord, measuring up to the full and complete standard of Christ. Then we will no longer be immature like children. We won't be tossed and blown about by every wind of new teaching. We will not be influenced when people try to trick us with lies so clever they sound like the truth. Instead, we will speak the truth in love, growing in every way more and more like Christ, who is the head of his body, the church.

---

a   1 Corinthians 13:6, Ephesians 4:15

He makes the whole body fit together perfectly. As each part does its own special work, it helps the other parts grow, so that the whole body is healthy and growing and full of love.

// Ephesians 4:13-16

We must speak the truth. But even in speaking truth, we must follow the Great Commandment. Speaking the truth doesn't create a loophole that allows us to be unloving. You may have been mad at me earlier when I mentioned the treatment of Muslims, the LGBT+ community or people you just may not like. You may feel entitled to be intolerant or unforgiving because of "truth." If you do that, you're leaving out the other part of the equation.

Yes, Jesus is truth. But he gave us a gift. Grace. This is the same gift that he wants us to give to other people.

The balance between grace and truth is love. That is what Paul brings to the forefront. We must speak the truth. But we must do so in such a way that people feel our love—and God's love too.

That's hard. Love requires care. Love requires empathy. Love requires a lot of things according to 1 Corinthians 13. Love requires that I connect with you before I correct you. Love requires that I make sure you understand how much I want what is best for you. Love requires that when I tell you the truth, I do so with the intent to help you, not hurt you.

Jesus was great at correction. He was also great at connection. Too many Christians make it their goal and purpose to "speak truth" and make love an afterthought. They want to correct people without connecting with them. Truth by itself is not loving, it's harsh. Jesus doesn't want truth or love. He wants both.

"When he saw the crowds, he had compassion on them because they were confused and helpless, like sheep without a shepherd."
// Matthew 9:36

Compassion there means to *"suffer with someone else."* Until we have compassion toward the "crowds" we face in life, the truth is ineffective.

Why is truth ineffective? Because the truth is only one half of a whole.

If our only goal is truth, we never get saved.

"But God is so rich in mercy, and he loved us so much, that even though we were dead because of our sins, he gave us life when he raised Christ from the dead. (It is only by God's grace that you have been saved!)"
// Ephesians 2:4-5

Being saved from the worst parts of ourselves only comes through grace. We must accept God's gift of grace, but we also must be willing to give that same gift. Truth doesn't save anyone. Only grace does. We all need grace.

If our only goal is grace, we never get free.

"And you will know the truth, and the truth will set you free."
// John 8:32

We need both. Grace saves us, but truth sets you free. And the way to strike the balance between them is to walk in love. That is hard. Some moments require grace, some require truth, all require love.

Anyone who hates another brother or sister is really a murderer at heart. And you know that murderers don't have eternal life within them. We know what real love is because Jesus gave up his life for us. So we also ought to give up our lives for our brothers and sisters. If someone has enough money to live well and sees a brother or sister in need but shows no compassion—how can God's love be in that person? Dear children, let's not merely say that we love each other; let us show the truth by our actions.

// 1 John 3:15-18

Do *they* need to change or do *you*?

There's a difference between following Jesus and believing in him. It's not just about eternity, it's about the kind of world that we create today. That's what Jesus was concerned with. People require compassion. To follow Jesus is to act like him.

We shouldn't really focus on *them*. That's been the problem all along. You may have read this and thought, "that's right." If so many of us feel this way, why aren't we making more progress? Because the focus is still on externals. Other people, Christians or not. *Them.* Some people or community *out there.* We think they are the ones who need to change. Not us.

But it's not about them, is it? It's about you, and it's about me. How well are we doing at this? You may be a Christian; you may not be. One thing we can agree on is that the world is a better place when people are more loving and more compassionate. Are you that person? Maybe *they* will never change. But you can. I can. There will always be a problem. There will always be a *them.* We don't have to be part of the problem. We can be part of the solution. That requires us to exert a remarkable amount of control over our internals and practice equanimity every day. Because the only person we can force to be more loving is ourselves.

This way of love is simple to understand. Simple ≠ easy. That's why we have the New Testament. It challenges us and gives us a glimpse into why this matters so much. It shows us, primarily through the life of Jesus, that God so loved the world. And it tells us that we can too, no matter how messy it is.

This is the invitation. Not to be a Christian, but to follow Jesus in doing this. To have the same thoughts, attitudes and actions that he had. Grace, truth, love.

This is why we need to know God. This is why we need to have faith in his plan, in Jesus. This is why we need to live by virtue. Because those are the tools that help us to love the world and, therefore, change it for the better.

Everything we have learned up to this point is meant to help us in applying this one commandment to our life.

Don't just say it, live it. It will take every ounce of who you are to do this. To do this, you must have a personal understanding of how much God loves you, and you must let go of what you cannot control. You must have virtues, and you must decide that your life is about much more than you.

Why are the rules so important? Because every person should feel the same love that God expresses toward us. If we don't live by the Great Commandment, we will live a life that is unloving. We will most certainly make the world around us a worse place.

If we decide to live by the rules, we should understand that God intends for us to make a positive impact on everyone we meet. We are meant to make the world a better place. Sometimes "the world" is the person standing right in front of us or commenting on our social media.

This requires deep work. Theology and philosophy intersect to help us do everything we can to play our part in the plan.

21 // THE TREASURE

"The following day John was again standing with two of his disciples. As Jesus walked by, John looked at him and declared, 'Look! There is the Lamb of God!' When John's two disciples heard this, they followed Jesus. Jesus looked around and saw them following. 'What do you want?' he asked them. They replied, 'Rabbi' (which means 'Teacher'), 'where are you staying?' 'Come and see,' he said. It was about four o'clock in the afternoon when they went with him to the place where he was staying, and they remained with him the rest of the day."

// John 1:35-39

These verses in John take place right after Jesus is baptized by John the Baptist. As we have seen, the logos—the plan of God—becomes a person, Jesus. Jesus is then identified by John as the final sacrifice to cover all sin. Other people start to recognize that fact, and Jesus asks them to follow him. These people become known as disciples.

It's simple: they believed and then they followed. They saw Jesus, believed in who he was, and decided to follow him wherever he went. They sought to follow and adopt his way of living. Many scholars believe that Seneca and Jesus were the same age. Musonius Rufus would have been a teenager during Jesus' lifetime. The Stoicism these men demonstrated brought many followers. Similarly, Jesus had a group of people around him seeking to understand and live his philosophy of life.

Someone part of a certain school of philosophy would call their teacher *didaskalos* (διδάσκαλος). This word means *master* or *teacher*. When referring to Jesus, the disciples in the New Testament used this same word to describe Jesus.

Is that to say that Jesus' goal was to found a school of philosophy? No. That's thinking too small. Jesus' goal was to change the world with a new way of thinking and living that people had never seen before.

Many Christians think that they have it figured out. They tell us about how Jesus wants us to be Christians. That's the goal, to be a believer in Jesus. They treat faith and salvation like they are the end goal. Church services are oriented around "salvation experiences." Most churches, especially in the west, see "salvations" as the ultimate measure of effectiveness.

Accepting the gift of grace is one of the most important things that we will ever do. Salvation, however, is not the goal. It's the start of the journey. But too many Christians get this wrong. People ask, "Are you saved?" Once they get someone "saved," or once they themselves are "saved," they believe their life will be good because their eternity is secure.

Why then do so many Christians have bad lives? Why are so many of those who claim to be "saved" so bad at living? Dysfunction, drama, and discontentment are just as present in the lives of most Christians as they are in those who are not "saved." Faith makes us right with God, but faith doesn't give us the ability to live life right.

In 2010, eighty-year-old Forrest Fenn, a former Air Force pilot and art collector hid a treasure chest somewhere in the Rocky Mountains. A mountain range in North America that stretches three thousand miles from New Mexico to northern Canada. This forty-pound treasure chest contained gold, rare coins, jewelry, diamonds, emeralds, rubies and sapphires. The value of this treasure has been estimated around two million dollars.

He wrote a book, *The Thrill of the Chase*, and the stories in the book were claimed to contain hints to where to find the treasure. Specifically, there was a poem with nine clues supposed to function like a map to help seekers find the treasure. The treasure was out there somewhere, and people were determined to find it. As many as 350,000 people searched for this treasure, and five died in their search.

Ten years later, on June 6, 2020, the treasure had been found. Fenn passed away six months later in September of 2020. The finder was **Jack Stuef**, a thirty-two-year-old medical student. This was how he described his find:

> *"The moment it happened [the treasure was found] was not the triumphant Hollywood ending some surely envisioned; it just felt like I had just survived something and was fortunate to come out the other end. For so long, I thought I might be haunted for the rest of my days by knowing where the treasure was but being unable to find it. Would I still be out there in that section of forest 50 years from now looking for it? When I finally found it, the primary emotion was not joy but rather the most profound feeling of relief in my entire life.* [60]

Jesus himself compares his Kingdom to a treasure:

> *"The Kingdom of Heaven is like a treasure that a man discovered hidden in a field. In his excitement, he hid it again and sold everything he owned to get enough money to buy the field."*
> **// Matthew 13:44**

It's not enough to believe treasure exists. The seeker must do everything they can to find that treasure—whatever it may be for you.

Believing in treasure is the first step to taking the journey to find treasure. But belief in treasure does not mean that it is within our possession. Moreover, our possession of treasure does not mean we see it as valuable. You may say, "If I had treasure worth two million dollars, I would definitely value it." Are you sure? What if you didn't know what two million dollars could buy? What if you didn't have a concept of money or value?

Earlier in this book, we talked about how there's a difference between pyrite and real gold. What if we treat real gold like its pyrite? The first documented discovery of gold in the United States was made by twelve-year-old Conrad Reed in 1799. He pulled a seventeen-pound gold nugget from a creek in North Carolina.

Gold is worth $2000 per ounce today. That means Conrad Reed pulled $544,000 in today's money out of a creek. Not knowing its value, his family used the gold nugget as a doorstop for several years. They then sold it to a local jeweler for $3.50. It's true worth in 1799 would have been $3,600—1,000 times what they sold it for.

The largest pearl ever found was found by a Filipino fisherman around 2006. The seventy-five-pound pearl is one foot wide and two feet long. He took it home and hid it under his bed as a good luck charm. It stayed under his bed for more than ten years. The fisherman had forgotten about it until he was moving out of his home. He gave it to a relative for safekeeping because he considered it too large to move to his new home. It is estimated that this pearl could be worth over $100 million.[61]

Treasure is only treasure if we decide it is.

A kingdom is any place where there is a sovereign ruler who has absolute authority and influence. Jesus calls his philosophy his way of living the kingdom of God. Why? To be dramatic? It was to draw the distinction between a belief system and a way of life. Jesus was not inviting the disciples to follow him so that they would believe in him. They made the choice to believe in him on their own.

He was inviting them into a way of life ruled by him that would change everything about their existence. It's more than grace, more than forgiveness, and more than belief. It's bigger than our own self-interest—grander than trying to create a world that fits our politics or religion. To decide to follow means to submit to a kingdom. To live a life of self-denial, not self-preservation.

This kingdom is about living life for the sake of, and in service to, everyone around us. This is called discipleship. Being a follower of Jesus means that we become disciples of him. We learn and submit to his teachings and leadership. There are some Christians who do this. Their belief is much more than belief; it affects everything about their way of life. These people are all too often the exception, not the rule.

If we call ourselves followers of Jesus, living life like him should not be optional. It should be our requirement. When Jesus asked his disciples to "come and see," he asked them to become his apprentices. He asks the same of us. He asks us to learn how to live our life as though he were the one living it. If he were a CEO, what kind of CEO would he be? If he were a parent to your children, what kind of parent would he be?

Jesus means to take ordinary people and change their lives, and thus change the world.

For Abraham, it was all about faith—acting based on his belief. Too often in Christianity, belief is preached as the finish line when it is supposed to be the start. Believing in Jesus is like having the treasure map in your hand. You don't have the treasure yet, you've got to work to find it.

> *You say you have faith, for you believe that there is one God. Good for you! Even the demons believe this, and they tremble in terror. How foolish! Can't you see that faith without good deeds is useless? Don't you remember that our ancestor Abraham was shown to be right with God by his actions when he offered his son Isaac on the altar? You see, his faith and his actions worked together. His actions made his faith complete. And so it happened just as the Scriptures say: "Abraham believed God, and God counted him as righteous because of his faith." He was even called the friend of God. So you see, we are shown to be right with God by what we do, not by faith alone.*

// James 2:19-24

By believing, we receive God's gift of grace that makes us part of his family. It's not good deeds that get us into heaven. But the good things we do are the completion of our faith. God wants us to act like Abraham. Believing isn't special. Anyone can believe. It takes a life of virtue to have faith.

Doing this is simple, but simple ≠ easy.

Author **Bill Hull** says it this way, *"follow Jesus, and he will teach you everything you need to know."* [62]

Grace guarantees our eternity. It's a free gift after all, and all we have to do is believe. Grace, however, doesn't guarantee a good life. Grace doesn't mean that we will be successful. Grace doesn't mean we will have good relationships with people around us. Grace doesn't mean we will not be dysfunctional. Grace doesn't guarantee that we will leave this world any better than we found it. Only following Jesus can do that.

Churches are full of believers. They are also full of followers. Followers of politics, self-interest, culture and other countless agendas. The world doesn't need another "Christian." The world needs someone to be like Jesus. That's what the New Testament is for. It teaches us how to follow Jesus. Not just how to believe, but how to live. Everything has led to this moment, learning how to live like Jesus. This is the ultimate philosophy of life—a way of life that has the potential to change the essence of our world.

In Matthew 28, Jesus asks those who follow him to teach other people to follow him. This is what we are supposed to do: understand how much God loves us, act in love—like Jesus did—and teach other people to do the same.

This is where knowing God and living out a philosophy of life can help us. We have a framework by which to apply these things to our life.

This is in fact what God has wanted us to do all along.

Don't copy the behavior and customs of this world, but let God transform you into a new person by changing the way you think. Then you will learn to know God's will for you, which is good and pleasing and perfect.

// Romans 12:2

Everything for us, and for God, starts with our thinking. If we can change our thinking, we can change our attitudes, if we can change our attitudes, we can change our actions.

This is how we work. And this is how God chooses to work with us. We are striving to know God's will for our lives, solving the great question of meaning. God gives us the answer: to be good philosophers.

To be a good philosopher, we must think better. We must use every ounce of our thinking to bring our feelings and attitudes under control. We must do good things. These good things must emulate the way of Jesus, the way of love. And if we can do this, and teach other people as well, we will find meaning and live a good life.

It's not enough to believe. It's not enough to be saved.

We must demonstrate our belief through our life. We must make the world better through our thoughts, attitudes and actions. That's what Jesus would do.

22// THE SPIRIT - PART 1

So God created human beings in his own image. In the image of God he created them; male and female he created them.

// Genesis 1:27

Then the Lord God formed the man from the dust of the ground. He breathed the breath of life into the man's nostrils, and the man became a living person.

// Genesis 2:7

What makes a person a person? Most of us have come to understand that there are three distinct things that come together to form a person: spirit, soul and body.

Body
The physical part of who we are. Our five senses and our physical matter. The eleven main systems of the human body fuse to form the matter of our physical presence.

Soul
The center of our mind, will, and emotions. All our thinking and feeling occurs within our soul. Our desires are centered within our soul. We know that we have a mind, will and emotions, but these things don't seem to have a physical location; nevertheless, people have attempted to locate the physical place of the soul since the beginning of recorded history. Our mind, emotions and will are unique to us, and we are aware of this uniqueness. It is hard for us to understand where this uniqueness comes from; therefore, we call

it a soul. It is the non-physical part of our everyday life: thoughts, emotions and desires that can't be easily quantified or divided into systems like our physical body can.

Spirit

But we are not just a body and a soul. There is something deeper within us that is transcendent—something spiritual that goes beyond our human experience.

There is something in us that looks beyond ourselves and wonders why. Why are we here? Why does anything exist? The ability to look beyond ourselves is a uniquely human characteristic. The notion that life is supposed to be meaningful drives us to look for meaning. It's as if we know intuitively that our individual selves are not enough. We have a thirst that will never be quenched until we connect with something greater than ourselves.

> *"If I find in myself desires which nothing in this world can satisfy, the only logical explanation is that I was made for another world."* [63]
>
> **// C.S. Lewis**

There is something within us that tells us that we are more than our body. Much more than our soul. There is something that lies beyond our finite and personal experience. We have a sense of the infinite. There is something more than "human" about us. There is no other being on the planet that possesses this desire for more.

Human beings are the only things that are created in God's image. What specifically is created in God's image? Our body? The first human body was formed out of dirt. God doesn't have a physical body that we know of. If he did, how would we explain how different humanity looks across the earth? Could our soul be the thing formed in God's image? Romans 12 tells us that God wants to transform us into a new person by changing the way we think. Isaiah 55 tells us that God's thoughts are higher than our thoughts, higher than heaven is above earth. So, we can rule out our mind, will and emotions being in the image of God.

Genesis 2 tells us that God himself breathed the breath of life into humanity. The ancient Stoics used a Greek word *pneuma* (πνεῦμα) to define this *breath of life*. In Stoic thought, the pneuma is the animating force of life. It drives both our body and soul. This pneuma doesn't just animate the individual person; it is the animating force of the universe. Our individual pneuma connects with the pneuma of the logos. The divine plan and reason is also the thing that animates us. The spirit of God made our spirit in his own image.

There is something within us that makes us alive. This is our spirit, our pneuma. The New Testament uses this same word to describe the spirit, not just the spirit of a person but the Spirit of God. All of humanity that lives has taken their first breath. The breath of life.

Our spirit is our animating force. The best and most pure part of us. It is the core of our personhood. It is our connection to other people and to the eternal. It is a gift from God that makes us more than just a body and a soul. It represents the image of God within us. Our spirit is what makes us more than animals. The spirit is the gift that God gave only to us that is meant to transcend our human experience, to connect back to him and to other people. This is the likeness of God within us.

Our spirit is the core thing that makes us us. It ties our body and soul together and is the driving force for both. It is the core and eternal part of every human being.

"We are not human beings having a spiritual experience. We are

spiritual beings having a human experience." [64]

// **Wayne W. Dyer**

We are spiritual beings. We are not just meant to contextualize our life based on our physical experiences or our thoughts, feelings and desires. Our spirit is the seat of our being, who we are at our core. The breath of God that gives each one of us life at the moment of our creation.

This spirit is a gift from God. It is the thing that defines our existence. It represents a unique part of God that he has given to each one of us individually and uniquely.

A long time ago, my dad, Keith Craft, came up with an exercise. In fact, he wrote a book on it titled *Your Divine Fingerprint*. I'll paraphrase that book and exercise briefly:

> Look at your hand. Look at your fingers. What's on the end of your fingertips? A fingerprint. Science tells us that our fingerprint is unique only to us. There has never been anyone else in history with your fingerprint. There will never be anyone in the future with your fingerprint. Your fingerprint is a physical manifestation of your spirit. A unique expression of God himself. On your body is a physical representation of this uniqueness in your fingerprint.
>
> Three months before you are born, your fingerprints are fully developed in the womb. So, not only do you have a fingerprint, you have a fingerprint that God himself gave to you the moment he created you. Ask yourself this question: What's the purpose of your fingerprint? Why would God give you, and only you, the fingerprint that he gave you?
>
> According to Jesus in John 17, there is a glory that he has given you. God's glory is not an attribute that he possesses but it is

the way he reveals himself to the world. You have the power within you to reveal who God is to the world. That's what your fingerprint represents; that's what your spirit represents. Think about it. You leave a fingerprint on everything you physically touch. Couldn't there also be a fingerprint that God wants to leave on the world through you?[65]

All of this starts with our spirit. Understanding the power of our divine fingerprint.

Think of a $100 bill. We all know a $100 bill is worth $100. If you crumple that $100 in your hand, how much is it worth? If you drop it on the ground and step on it with your shoe, how much is it worth?

Our body may experience physical pain and hindrance. Our souls may experience difficulty and torment. But if we understand that there is a part of us that is meant to connect back to God himself, and live our life with this understanding, our worth will never be determined by anything external.

Our true worth will be determined by our understanding that we have a *"fingerprint [spirit] that no one else has; to leave an imprint that no one else can leave."* [66]

We have been given a spirit. This spirit doesn't just animate our soul and body. This spirit drives us to live a life that is beyond our present experience.

23 // THE SPIRIT - PART 2

Our soul represents our thinking, attitudes, and desires. Our body represents our actions and the physical consequences—good and bad—of our actions. Our thinking and perspectives must come from somewhere. Those things must originate from something beyond our body and soul. Ultimately, our soul and bodies are followers of our spirit.

Every person who ever has or ever will walk this planet has a spirit. Having a spirit may give us a sense of morality. It may give us a conscience. It may help us understand that there is life beyond the present. But there is no guarantee that we will live a good life simply because we become aware that we have a spirit, soul, and body.

If each person on this planet has a spirit that connects back to God, how do we explain the evil we see in our world? There are people who walk the face of this world and perpetuate evil acts, despite God creating them in his image. There are people who treat others with contempt and refuse to see them as created in God's image.

Socrates and Plato believed that people are born good and that as we go through life, we forget our basic goodness.[67] We begin to do what is wrong and think that it is right. To counteract that, we must seek wisdom and virtue in philosophy, and only by those things can we attain moral goodness. Through philosophy we remind ourselves of what true moral goodness is.

The ancient Stoics believed that good and evil were purely personal judgments and principles. We cannot truly know what is objectively good, only what is good to us, and what is good to us is living by the virtues we select. They believe the evil we do is because of our inability to live by virtue, and the goodness or evil of others is not our concern because that is not within our control.

Many philosophical explanations for the battle of good and evil within us fall short. Are we inherently good, evil, or somewhere in between? This is an eternal question we have asked since the beginning of time.

Are human beings inherently good? Did you teach your children to lie? To disobey? Or to be selfish? We do not teach these things to our children. We go to great lengths to teach them not to be selfish, disobedient, and untruthful. These things are not taught to our children; they are already within their nature.

Our bodies and even our souls are naturally drawn to sin, making mistakes on purpose. Why? Paul says in Romans 5, sin has been part of our nature since Adam and Eve in the garden. All of us have sinned and are sinful. Our flesh—our physical body—is sinful; our entire bodies are ruled by sin, as Paul tells us throughout his writing..

> *"Do not love this world nor the things it offers you, for when you love the world, you do not have the love of the Father in you. For the world offers only a craving for physical pleasure, a craving for everything we see, and pride in our achievements and possessions. These are not from the Father, but are from this world."*
>
> **// 1 John 2:15-16**

All of us have physical cravings. We have appetites for food, fun, experiences and even people. The more we pursue these things, the worse we often feel. Eating a whole large pizza sounds like a great idea, until after we eat it. Many people enjoy alcohol to excess, until the hangover. Pornography and promiscuity attract us until we are flooded with regret. We think physical cravings will satisfy us, but they are empty calories. We eat plenty but find ourselves malnourished.

We have cravings in our soul: desires for significance, achievement, influence, wealth and what the world calls success. Filling ourselves with these things only increases our hunger. Without proper nutrition, we experience all kinds of illnesses.

What does our spirit crave? Purpose, meaning, a connection to God himself. We often think that by pursuing the cravings of our body and soul that our spirit will be satisfied. That is never true.

"Humans can reproduce only human life, but the Holy Spirit gives birth to spiritual life."

// John 3:6

Our spirit may come from God himself, but what about our body and soul? Science tells us that our physical traits are inherited from our parents. They got theirs from their parents and so on, all the way to Adam and Eve.

What about our soul? Our thinking, attitudes and actions? The world around us does a great job of shaping those. Our parents, upbringing, culture, societal expectations, wealth and environment shape most of what we feel about the world. This often happens long before we could process these things maturely.

Because of its intangible nature, we tend to neglect our spirit. We listen more often to our body and soul. We think that satisfying our body's and soul's cravings will fulfill the longing of our spirit. But that is the road to nowhere.

God knew that. Jesus did too. Remember that philosophy is merely choosing the best way for us to live. Jesus invites us into living life his way and following him. His first followers could talk with him face to face and be coached along the way. He trained them himself in his philosophy. That's what great philosophers do. They don't just teach a philosophy, they live one, and they actively direct, correct and encourage others to do the same.

Jesus' biblical story concludes with his final sacrifice and resurrection to bring about God's plan. Once he was resurrected, he left the earth and his disciples. But he didn't just leave them to themselves. He promised to send a helper, an advocate. The New Testament calls this helper the Holy Spirit.

"If you love me, obey my commandments. And I will ask the Father, and he will give you another Advocate, who will never leave you. He is the Holy Spirit, who leads into all truth. The world cannot receive him, because it isn't looking for him and doesn't recognize him. But you know him, because he lives with you now and later will be in you. No, I will not abandon you as orphans—I will come to you. [19] Soon the world will no longer see me, but you will see me. Since I live, you also will live. When I am raised to life again, you will know that I am in my Father, and you are in me, and I am in you. Those who accept my commandments and obey them are the ones who love me. And because they love me, my Father will love them. And I will love them and reveal myself to each of them."

// John 14:15-21

That term *Holy Spirit* may sound strange. It's not a term you would probably hear outside of a church. It seems mystical and foreign. Let's remind ourselves that we are more than just human beings living in a physical world. Our human form is driven by a spirit longing for connection to something more than what we see and feel.

You and Jiminy Cricket

We should strive to resist the cravings of the body and soul. We should embrace the cravings of the spirit and allow those cravings to lead us to the Holy Spirit.

This is what we speak, not in words taught us by human wisdom but in words taught by the Spirit, explaining spiritual realities with Spirit-taught words. The person without the Spirit does not accept the things that come from the Spirit of God but considers them foolishness, and cannot understand them because they are discerned only through the Spirit.

// 1 Corinthians 2:13-14 NIV

It's not just our spirit. It's the Spirit. The Stoics believed that our pneuma was our connection to the logos. Our spirit is our connection to the Holy Spirit. It is the thing about us that is created in God's image to connect back to him.

God didn't intend for us to live our lives alone. We aren't on a solitary spiritual journey to fulfillment. When Jesus was here, he was a helper for his disciples. He guided them and convicted them when they made mistakes. At the end of his time with them, Jesus tells his disciples that he is leaving a helper to help them. We use the term Holy Spirit to describe the helper that Jesus has sent to walk through life with us and help us, guide us and make us aware of what we need to do at certain times.

The Holy Spirit works in our lives a lot like Jiminy Cricket does in the movie *Pinocchio*, trying to keep us off the wrong track and on the right track. Again, the theologians are angry. Call it a feeling, a voice or a leading. The Holy Spirit is who confirms in us the truth of who Jesus is and helps us live a good life by following him. When we decide to follow Jesus, the Holy Spirit begins to lead us and walk alongside us through life. In John 16, Jesus says that the Holy Spirit convicts us of our sins. Being convicted and being led are two different experiences. People can be convicted but still refuse to listen. Just like Pinocchio and Jiminy Cricket. To be convicted is to become aware of how our sin separates us from God. This is stronger than our conscience, shame, or guilt. Conviction is the realization that our sin will prevent our spirit from ever being connected to the God that created it. Conviction makes us aware of the futility of our self-righteousness. Through conviction, the Holy Spirit invites us to accept Jesus' gift of grace.

To allow the Holy Spirit to lead us, we give him the steering wheel of our life. When the Holy Spirit leads our spirit, we make changes in our own life based on our convictions. The Holy Spirit is much more than Jiminy Cricket. To be led by the Holy Spirit is to allow God to transform you into a new person my changing your thoughts, attitudes, and actions. Following Jesus requires the Holy Spirit. Our spirit being led by the Holy Spirit requires us to follow Jesus.

Believing in Jesus is simple. Following him is hard. Simple ≠ easy. That's why we need help from the Holy Spirit. Jesus tells us to love our neighbor as ourselves. This is a simple concept, but the state of the world reflects how difficult it is to live out this concept.

Yes, we have a spirit that is created in God's image, but we have a choice to make regarding our spirit. In Romans chapters seven and eight, the apostle Paul spells out this tension.

> *I don't really understand myself, for I want to do what is right, but I don't do it. Instead, I do what I hate. But if I know that what I am doing is wrong, this shows that I agree that the law is good.*
>
> **// Romans 7:15-16**

210

We often feel this way, don't we? We know what to do and we want to do it, but we do the things we know we shouldn't do. This is part of having a human experience. We are all predisposed to sin, to miss the mark. If we decide to follow Jesus, it's not just about accepting his story or our role in God's plan. It's about understanding that to play our role, we need to be more like Jesus in how we live. We need to turn from our body's and soul's cravings to true spiritual fulfillment. This can only happen when we allow the Holy Spirit to lead our spirit.

So now there is no condemnation for those who belong to Christ Jesus. And because you belong to him, the power of the life-giving Spirit has freed you from the power of sin that leads to death. The law of Moses was unable to save us because of the weakness of our sinful nature. So God did what the law could not do. He sent his own Son in a body like the bodies we sinners have. And in that body God declared an end to sin's control over us by giving his Son as a sacrifice for our sins. He did this so that the just requirement of the law would be fully satisfied for us, who no longer follow our sinful nature but instead follow the Spirit.

Those who are dominated by the sinful nature think about sinful things, but those who are controlled by the Holy Spirit think about things that please the Spirit. So letting your sinful nature control your mind leads to death. But letting the Spirit control your mind leads to life and peace. For the sinful nature is always hostile to God. It never did obey God's laws, and it never will. That's why those who are still under the control of their sinful nature can never please God.

But you are not controlled by your sinful nature. You are controlled by the Spirit if you have the Spirit of God living in you. (And remember that those who do not have the Spirit of Christ living in them do not belong to him at all.)

// Romans 8:1-9

The nature within each one of us is drawn to sin. It's part of being human. We have a body, we have a soul. It is natural to want to give in to what our soul and body desire. There is a spirit within each one of us that God has created. The Spirit of God is meant to guide our spirit. This Holy Spirit doesn't merely help us "not sin." If we choose to follow the Spirit, and therefore Jesus, we will live a good life no matter what our external situation looks like.

Explaining the unexplainable

How does the Holy Spirit work? Once we choose to follow Jesus, do we all get superpowers like spiritual wizards? Do we forget about our body's or spirit's cravings?

The Holy Spirit operates in unexplainable ways. The New Testament teaches us that there are gifts and abilities that the Holy Spirit can and will give us. Many of the churches I grew up in made these gifts of the Spirit a priority. It can be easy to place a priority on spiritual gifts since they can encourage, strengthen and comfort us. However, spiritual gifts are not Christian superpowers, nor are they the primary proof of the Holy Spirit working in our lives.

When we decide to follow Jesus and live like him, we must also learn how to be convicted by his values. We should allow the Bible to shape the virtues we live by. We need to allow our spirit—our pneuma, what animates and drives us—to be led by God's Spirit so our soul and body can reflect God's plan for the world—the logos.

The majority of the New Testament shows us how the Holy Spirit means to work in our lives to lead us and guide us to be like Jesus. We must remember as we read the stories of the New Testament that we are not human beings having spiritual experiences, but spiritual beings having human experiences.[68] It is essential that we allow our spirit to be governed by the plan and purpose of God. That must be our highest aim.

So put to death the sinful, earthly things lurking within you. Have nothing to do with sexual immorality, impurity, lust, and evil desires. Don't be greedy, for a greedy person is an idolater, worshiping the things of this world.

// Colossians 3:5

Paul tells us to not just ignore our cravings but to put them to death—bury them in the ground and walk away forever.

God wants us to live a good life. That is his plan. He means for your life to have impact beyond itself. We must understand who he is, who we are and the role we play to do that. To play our part well, we must allow our spirit to listen to his Spirit.

Fruit tastes better than gifts

It's not enough to believe. The real question we should ask when living our lives is the effectiveness question: "How is that working out for you?"

If you're a Jesus follower and you're reading this, how is following Jesus working out for you? Is your life better, worse or the same as it was before?

In John 15, Jesus tells us that if we follow him well, we will bear fruit. Throughout the Gospels, he tells us that there is good fruit and bad fruit in nature, so there is good fruit and bad fruit in humanity.

But the Holy Spirit produces this kind of fruit in our lives: love, joy, peace, patience, kindness, goodness, faithfulness, gentleness, and self-control. There is no law against these things! Those who belong to Christ Jesus have nailed the passions and desires of their sinful nature to his cross and crucified them there. Since we are living by the Spirit, let us follow the Spirit's leading in every part of our lives.

// Galatians 5:22–25

Jesus has added us to the covenant, to Abraham's family. He is asking us to go produce fruit. Jesus says,

You didn't choose me. I chose you. I appointed you to go and produce lasting fruit, so that the Father will give you whatever you ask for, using my name.

// John 15:16

The question is not "What do I believe?" it is "What is the fruit of my belief?"

When we decide to follow Jesus, the Holy Spirit works with us to help us understand real virtue. True virtue is created by God and shown to us in Scripture. As we understand virtue, the Holy Spirit helps our thoughts, attitudes and actions align with the virtues of God. Our gifts, spirit, soul, and body work together to produce this fruit. This is where philosophy and theology can come together to equip us to live a life of purpose, meaning and impact. A good life.

The gifts of the Spirit are gifts; we don't have to work for them. Each of us have gifts based on who we are and who God wants us to be. We should not make these our priority. Our priority should be demonstrating the fruit of the Spirit in our thoughts, attitudes, and actions. Jesus tells us in John 15 he chose us to bear fruit, not operate in gifts. Gifts are important and gifts are great. But gifts are not our goal. Fruit is.

All of us should have convictions. But we should have the right ones. We should have virtues, and those virtues should be God's virtues. When we live by our conviction to follow Jesus, we are listening to the leading of the Holy Spirit. The Holy Spirit can and will help us to live a life of virtue. This doesn't mean we get superpowers. It means we have help to live the life we're designed for.

The Stoics had it mostly right: We should live a life of virtue. We should focus on what we can control, not what we can't. We should deeply consider our thoughts, attitudes, and actions. And we should do this so we can live a good life and make a great impact on those closest to us.

Stoicism is a powerful tool, but we need more than a philosophy. Knowing ourselves is just one part of our journey. We need a relationship with the maker of the plan—God. We need to follow the plan that became a person—Jesus. And to do this, we must allow ourselves to be led by the Holy Spirit to produce good fruit.

24 // THE NEW FAMILY

"We cannot choose our parents, but we can choose whose children we become." // **Seneca**

We can't do this journey by ourselves. Abraham had a family. Jesus invited us into his family. So, we should be on this journey with other people.

These words are said to be written on the tombstone of a bishop in the crypt of Westminster Abbey,

> *When I was young and free and my imagination had no limits. I dreamed of changing the world.*

> *As I grew older and wiser, I discovered the world would not change.*

> *So I shortened my sights somewhat and decided to change only my country.*

> *But it too seemed immovable.*

> *As I grew into my twilight years, in one last desperate attempt I settled for changing only my family, those closest to me.*

> *But alas, they would have none of it.*

> *And now as I lay on my deathbed, I suddenly realize:*

If I had only changed myself first.

Then, by example I would have changed my family.

From their inspiration and encouragement, I would then have been able to better my country.

And who knows, I may even have changed the world.[69]

We should work hard on ourselves. After all, we can only control what we can control. But we are meant to change the world. To change the world, we need to surround ourselves with people who want to do the same thing. Jesus didn't come to the earth and live life alone. Ancient Stoics encouraged living by virtue so we can engage with those around us and make the world a better place. For our lives to be meaningful, we must mean something to those closest to us; a life cannot be meaningful on its own. The most meaningful relationships that we have are what we often call family. None of us had any control regarding the family we were born into. The most important family that we can have is the one we choose.

No one I know married their sibling, or even their cousin. At least I hope not. They chose to start a family with someone outside the family they were born into. They will have children and raise them as the family they have chosen.

Abraham had his relationship with God, so did his son Isaac, so did his son Jacob. All of them had their own choices to make regarding their relationships and the people they lived with.

God wants to work in the context of a family. Not just families of origin like Abraham's but families of choice. In Mark 3, Jesus calls "anyone who does God's will" his family. Anyone who wants to be in the family is in.

He actually gives his family a new commandment.

This is my commandment: Love each other in the same way I have loved you. There is no greater love than to lay down one's life for one's friends. You are my friends if you do what I command. I no longer call you slaves, because a master doesn't confide in his slaves. Now you are my friends, since I have told you everything the Father told me. You didn't choose me. I chose you. I appointed you to go and produce lasting fruit, so that the Father will give you whatever you ask for, using my name. This is my command: Love each other.

// John 15:12-17

When Jesus says *friends*, he uses the word *philos* (φιλος) which is the same word used when describing brotherly love. Jesus surrounded himself with people who became his family—disciples.

Throughout Scripture, God shows us the importance of finding our tribe, creating a family of choice around us committed to helping each other follow his plan, helping each other follow Jesus.

This family must be defined by their love for each other. They love each other (and others) like God loves them. That's the meaning and purpose for all of us. For us to lay down our ways, preferences and agendas to love people like we know God loves us.

We must take this journey. To know God, to know ourselves and then decide to play a role in God's plan. That's the only way to live a good life. A life of meaning and virtue.

God's new family

In Matthew 16, Jesus is asking his disciples about these things. He asks them what the word on the street is concerning his identity. Did people think he was just another rabbi, a teacher or perhaps a zealot? After hearing a variety of answers, Jesus did this:,

> *Then he asked them, "But who do you say I am?" Simon Peter answered, "You are the Messiah, the Son of the living God." Jesus replied, "You are blessed, Simon son of John, because my Father in heaven has revealed this to you. You did not learn this from any human being.*
>
> **// Matthew 16:15-17**

Peter was beginning to understand who God was, and who Jesus was. This was so powerful to Jesus (and Simon) that Jesus changed his name to Peter—just like God changed Abraham's name. Peter said Jesus was the Messiah, the logos, the fulfillment of God's plan.

> *Now I say to you that you are Peter (which means 'rock'), and upon this rock I will build my church, and all the powers of hell will not conquer it.*
>
> **// Matthew 16:18**

Just like the name Peter means *rock*, Peter's answer to Jesus' question is the foundation of a new family of people who believe this same thing—the church.

The word *church* in this passage is translated from the Greek word *ekklesia*. To the people Jesus was talking to, this was not a religious term. It described people gathering for a specific purpose. Any type of gathering—civic, military or otherwise—could be considered an ekklesia.

In this conversation, Jesus was announcing his plans to institute a new gathering, a unique assembly of people that represented a continuation of the family of Abraham. We all get to be in the family now.

The common ground of this new movement would not be a national, social, or political agenda. It would be him—the logos, the Messiah, the Son of the living God. This was going to be a gathering of people who believed that he was exactly who Peter declared him to be, those who chose to live like he did.

Jesus' declaration of building a movement must have sounded ridiculous to his disciples. It was just the twelve of them plus Jesus. But Jesus did exactly what he promised to do. Two thousand years later, these words are proof. Jesus' point was also unmistakable to his audience, not even the powers of hell, or his very death would stop the church.

After Jesus' death and resurrection, his followers were empowered to take his gospel into the streets of Jerusalem. There, in the city where he was crucified, the church was born. There were no buildings, no creeds, no Bible as we have it today. The church was a growing family of people who had one thing in common: they believed that Jesus was the Son of God, the plan made into a person, and that we should live like him.

25 // THE GIFTS

"There is no time for playing around. You have been retained as counsel for the unhappy. You have promised to bring help to the shipwrecked, the imprisoned, the sick, the needy, to those whose heads are under the poised axe. Where are you deflecting your attention? What are you doing?"

// **Seneca**

As Jesus' new family—the church—began to grow, people began to realize that each person had different personalities, gifts, and abilities.

In his grace, God has given us different gifts for doing certain things well. So if God has given you the ability to prophesy, speak out with as much faith as God has given you. If your gift is serving others, serve them well. If you are a teacher, teach well. If your gift is to encourage others, be encouraging. If it is giving, give generously. If God has given you leadership ability, take the responsibility seriously. And if you have a gift for showing kindness to others, do it gladly.

// **Romans 12:6-8**

They started to realize that the Holy Spirit didn't just want them to bear fruit. But based on their unique spirit, soul and body, God had given them gifts to be of service to their family and the world. Not only does God give us a fingerprint that no one else has, to leave an imprint no one else can leave, this fingerprint is meant to be a gift to the world. It is meant to help us understand and decide what the meaning of our life is and live that out every day.

Every person who follows Jesus should strive to demonstrate the fruit of the Spirit we discussed in Chapter 22. But there are unique abilities that everyone in the family gets to help each other. Paul says it this way:

> *"And the same is true for you. Since you are so eager to have the special abilities the Spirit gives, seek those that will strengthen the whole church."*
>
> **// 1 Corinthians 14:12**

Spiritual gifts are not natural abilities or character traits. They aren't titles or positions, although they may lead to that in some cases. Most importantly, our gifts are not about us, they are meant to be used to love people and point them toward God.

Jesus said in the book of Acts,

> *But you will receive power when the Holy Spirit comes upon you. And you will be my witnesses, telling people about me everywhere—in Jerusalem, throughout Judea, in Samaria, and to the ends of the earth.*
>
> **// Acts 1:8**

Ultimately, our gifts are meant to point people to the logos—to Jesus. They are meant to help people take the same journey we have taken. Our spirit, our gift and our fingerprint are not about us. As we have learned, to truly live a good life, we must decide what our life means to the people around us. The Holy Spirit gives us gifts so we can give those gifts to other people. If you're alive, you have gifts to give.

God reveals our gifts only in the context of relationships. That's why the family—the church—is so important. Without a family to give our gifts to, our gifts don't matter. After all, if you can't give a gift away, it's not a gift.

Why live a good life?

"The greatest gift you can give anyone is a healthy you." [70]

// **Keith Craft**

Why should we live a good life? Because our talents don't matter if we are unhealthy. Too many people want the world to tell them what they are worth. They are incapable of identifying their own value—the value that God has placed within them.

We must take the journey to know God, understand ourselves, and play a part in making the world a better place. If we can do this, we will be a gift to everyone we encounter. Every moment of our life will be filled with meaning and purpose. We may not get everything we want, but we will get (and give) the things that matter most.

God is not trying to convince us to join his religion. He's not concerned about getting us to believe a certain way. Jesus wasn't about founding an institution like a museum of faith.

Throughout history, God has been trying to help our lives mean something. He has been trying to get us on a journey with people who want their lives to mean something too. The church represents the hope of the world because God has always used people. The church is people, not a place. It is the home for our family of imperfect followers of Jesus. It is a place for us to learn and decide our philosophy, how we should live.

> **How will you measure your life?**
> **What do you want out of life?**
> **What is the meaning of your life?**

If you can learn to know God, and know yourself, only then can you see the part God designed only you to play. When you understand the role you are designed to play, every moment in your life will have meaning. Decide today what you want out of life and determine within yourself to live a good life—a life that changes the world.

∞ // THE FUTURE IS UNFINISHED

Merely learning these things will not do us any good unless we add them to our daily life.

There are a lot of people who believe in a lot of things, Christians included. The world doesn't need believers. The world needs people who live their beliefs.

Jesus gave us simple rules for life: love God with all our heart and then love all people like God loves us. It is hard to practice love like that when our spirit, soul, and body are so easily diverted and consumed by desires, passions, fears, and lusts for things outside of our control. The Stoics can help us learn and remember what is up to us and what is up to God alone.

> It is the Holy Spirit's job to convict people, God's job to judge, and my job to love." [71]
>
> **// Billy Graham**

We must remind ourselves of the role God has given us, which is simply to love people. That is within our control; the rest is up to God.

But we should also remember that not everyone knows what we know or is striving to live like we are. Remember the words of Marcus Aurelius:

> "When you wake up in the morning, tell yourself: The people I deal with today will be meddling, ungrateful, arrogant, dishonest, jeal-

ous, and surly. They are like this because they can't tell good from evil." [72]   // **Marcus Aurelius**

The only way to show people how to tell the difference between good and evil is to be good to them.

> *"...we know that "all of us possess knowledge." This "knowledge" puffs up, but love builds up. If anyone imagines that he knows something, he does not yet know as he ought to know."*
>
> // **1 Corinthians 8:1-2**

Now that we have decided to become good philosophers, let us live our philosophy more than we talk about it. Love is what will build people up, not our knowledge. Realize that you have not lived your whole life with this new philosophy, and you are far from it now.

Understanding how to live and striving to live are the hardest things we will ever do. The Navy SEALs teach us that "the only easy day was yesterday." It doesn't get easier, but the reward becomes clearer. Every day will be harder than the day before. We are built for this. God is faithful; he has a plan.

Now that we understand how to live, we must have the courage to give life, God, and others our life as a gift. We must strive—regardless of what is outside our control—to live our virtues. We are compelled, in every moment, to remind ourselves that true goodness only comes from controlling what we can control, the best way we can.

At the end of his journey on Earth, Jesus gave his followers a mission:

> *Jesus came and told his disciples, "I have been given all authority in heaven and on Earth. Therefore, go and make disciples of all the nations, baptizing them in the name of the Father and the Son*

and the Holy Spirit. Teach these new disciples to obey all the commands I have given you. And be sure of this: I am with you always, even to the end of the age

// Matthew 28:18-20

What is the meaning of life?

The goal of following Jesus is not to get us to believe better but to act better.

The New Testament uses the word *hagiasmos* (ἁγιασμός) to describe the journey of acting better. This word means to set something apart for the use intended by its designer. We can call this "holiness." If you've grown up in church, or been in church for a while, you may have heard the English word *sanctification*. A pen is sanctified when it is used to write. Eyeglasses are sanctified when they are used to help us see.

Holiness and sanctification are fancy words to describe something being set apart for its intended use.

Many people go their whole life and never decide what their life means. They never find themselves set apart for their intended use. This happens whether a person calls themselves a Christian or not. They never find people that help them find the way to live. They live in darkness and never discover or follow the plan that brings light into their life. Their life never brings light into the world. They never become sanctified. They are never used for what they were intended for.

In John 1, Jesus isn't just the logos, he's the *phos* (φῶς)—*the light.*

"The Word gave life to everything that was created, and his life brought light to everyone. The light shines in the darkness, and the darkness can never extinguish it."

// John 1:4-5

The life of Jesus represents what happens when we live a good life. Light enters a dark world. Jesus invites us to not just follow the plan but to be light like he is light. That is our intended use.

The meaning of our life is to be the light that only we can be, in every space we enter.

Living a life without meaning is like trying to find our way around in an unfamiliar, pitch-dark room. When we live meaningful lives, we bring light into the rooms we enter. In the history of humanity, no one had to "discover" light like we discovered electricity. Light has always existed. Every light has a source. Physically, humans have had to discover how to bring light into all kinds of dark rooms. We didn't create the sun, but we did create the light bulb and candle. Jesus is the source of light. The meaning that we make turns us into a light source. When we determine to be like Jesus, nothing can prevent us from making an impact on the world. The goal of living is to become a light like Jesus was and is.

"You are the light of the world—like a city on a hilltop that cannot be hidden. No one lights a lamp and then puts it under a basket. Instead, a lamp is placed on a stand, where it gives light to everyone in the house. In the same way, let your good deeds shine out for all to see, so that everyone will praise your heavenly Father."

// Matthew 5:14-16

Jesus himself was holy. He was used for his intended purpose during his time on Earth. We must also pursue holiness like Jesus did. Seek to be used by God. Seek holiness. We should see every day as a gift from God given to us to be used for his intended purpose.

As we do that, we must follow the plan—Jesus, the logos. As we become better at following the plan, we do good things, we live a good life. As we live a good life, the good things that we do are seen by everyone.

This good life, these good deeds, become light to the world.

Our light reflects our source of light, the logos, Jesus.

We now know God, we now know ourselves, and we've decided the role we want to play. Our journey doesn't stop there. We must let our light shine.

In John 8, Jesus brings our journey full circle. He asks the disciples, "Who do you say that I am?" It's one thing to know who God is because he tells you. It's another thing to say who God is through your own experiences. The journey God has us on is not solely meant to increase our understanding of him, or our knowledge of self. God intends for us to say who we know him to be for ourselves.

The disciples could do this, not because they knew a bunch of information but because they had been around Jesus every day. They knew exactly who he was because of their experiences with him. Their knowledge of God helped them know themselves. By knowing themselves, they could then play the role Jesus designed for them.

Jesus modeled the way to live for his disciples, and they in turn showed their disciples. This is why the church exists today. Throughout generations, disciples have given every ounce of effort they had to accomplish this mission with their time on Earth.

We must transition from student to master. This is God's plan. To play our part well, we must show others the way. The church shouldn't be full of believers, it should be full of disciples who are making disciples. That is the ultimate fulfillment of God's plan for all of us.

How are you going to teach other people to be part of the plan? How are you going to develop disciples?

> *"For the one who is tipping over cannot straighten up someone else, nor can the ignorant person teach, the disorderly establish order, the disorganized organize, the ungoverned govern."* [73]
>
> **// Plutarch**

We can't take people to a place that we've never been. For thousands of years, this Great Commission has been our mission. We've accomplished it with mixed results. Why? Because few people have ever had Jesus' mission become their mission.

It's not enough to believe in the plan. It's not enough to believe in the light. Our cause is to commit ourselves wholeheartedly to following the plan. We are meant to do good things that bring light to the world. We must do this so people can get out of their own personal darkness with Jesus' help.

Follow the plan, do good things, and your light will shine for the whole world to see.

> *But you should keep a clear mind in every situation. Don't be afraid of suffering for the Lord. Work at telling others the Good News, and fully carry out the ministry God has given you. As for me, my life has already been poured out as an offering to God. The time of my death is near. I have fought the good fight, I have finished the race, and I have remained faithful.*
>
> **// 2 Timothy 4:7**

God has given us all a role to play. Paul shows us that life is a fight, it's a race of endurance, and if we do our part well, we win. The world needs us to run our race with everything we have and bring people with us. If we finish, we are victorious.

> *So let's not get tired of doing what is good. At just the right time we will reap a harvest of blessing if we don't give up.*
> **// Galatians 6:9**

If doing good was easy, we wouldn't get weary. Don't forget that. Living this life is hard, being a disciple is hard, making disciples is hard, but there is greatness in store for us—and other people—if we don't quit. We are built for this battle.

> *"There is no grosser or greater misrepresentation of the Christian message than that which depicts it as offering a life of ease with no battle and struggle at all ... sooner or later every believer discovers that the Christian life is a battleground, not a playground.* [74]
> **// Dr. Martyn Lloyd-Jones**

Decide your dots.
Connect your dots.
Only worry about what is within your dots.

> *"Learning how to live takes a whole life, and, which may surprise you more, it takes a whole life to learn how to die."* **// Seneca**

APPENDIX A // SUPPLEMENTAL READING

If you're looking to delve further into Stoicism, the Bible, or developing a philosophy of life, these are great places to start.

Philosophy

Your Divine Fingerprint // *Keith Craft*

How to Be Free, The Enchiridion // *Epictetus, A. A. Long*

The Discourses // *Epictetus*

That One Should Disdain Hardships // *Musonius Rufus, Cora Lutz*

Meditations // *Marcus Aurelius, Gregory Hays*

Letters from a Stoic // *Seneca*

How to Think Like a Roman Emperor // *Donald Robertson*

A Guide to the Good Life // *William B. Irvine*

The Obstacle is the Way // *Ryan Holiday*

Lives of the Stoics // *Ryan Holiday*

How Will You Measure Your Life // *Clayton M. Christensen*

Man's Search for Meaning // *Viktor Frankl*

Works of Love // *Søren Kierkegaard*

Courage Under Fire // *James B. Stockdale*

Philosophy for Life and Other Dangerous Situations // *Jules Evans*

Theology/Following Jesus

Theology: An Introduction // *Alister McGrath*

A Popular Survey of the Old Testament // *Norman L. Geisler*

The Cost of Discipleship // *Dietrich Boenhoffer*

Simply Jesus // *N. T. Wright*

Conversion and Discipleship // *Bill Hull*

The Complete Book of Discipleship // *Bill Hull*

The Ragamuffin Gospel // *Brennan Manning*

Holy Fire // *R. T Kendall*

Mere Christianity // *C. S. Lewis*

Irresistible // *Andy Stanley*

An Unstoppable Force // *Erwin McManus*

The Spirit of the Disciplines // *Dallas Willard*

APPENDIX B // ART

An appendix of the art contained in the printed version.

0 // **The clumsy elephant,** *John Samuel Pughe, 1908*

1 // **The Sword of Damocles,** *Richard Westall, 1812*

2 // **Still Life with a Skull and a Writing Quill,** *Pieter Claesz, 1628*

3 // **The Bible of the Poor (Biblia Pauperum),** *Anonymous, 15th Century*

4 // **The Angels Appearing to Abraham,** *Francesco Guardi, 1750s*

5 // **Isaac Blessing Jacob,** *Gerbrand van den Eeckhout, 1642*

6 // **Ancient of Days Setting a Compass to the Earth,** *William Blake, 1794*

7 // **The Death of Socrates,** *Jacques Louis David, 1787*

8 // **Composizione,** *Piet Mondrian, 1916*

9 // **The School of Athens,** *Raphael, 1509–1511*

10 // **The Virgin and Child with Saints Jerome and Dominic,** *Filippino Lippi, 1485*

11 // **The Great Wave off Kanagawa,** *Hokusai, 1831*

12 // **Damaged Apollo 13 Module,** *NASA*

13 // **Al Capone and Easy Eddie**

14 // **James Stockdale in POW camp**

15 // **Altarpiece No. 1 Group X,** *Hilma af Klint, 1915*

16 // **The Baptism of Christ,** *Sebastiano Ricci, 1713–14*

17 // Paradise, *Carlo Saraceni, 1598*

18 // A scene of Hell, *Jan Brueghel The Elder*

19 // The Good Samaritan, *Rembrandt van Rijn, 1630*

20 // What is truth? Christ and Pilate, *Nikolai Nikolaevich Ge, 1890*

21 // The Treasure-seeker, *Theodor Matthias von Holst, 1840*

22 // Light Circle, *Wassily Kandinsky, 1922*

23 // Ezekiel's Vision, *Raphael, 1517–1518*

24 // The Triumph of the Church, *Peter Paul Rubens, 1626–1633*

25 // The Annunciation, *Botticelli (Alessandro di Mariano Filipepi), ca. 1485–92*

∞ // Turning Road (Route tournante), *Paul Cézanne, 1905*

ENDNOTES

Front Matter

1 *Lucius Annaeus Seneca, Natural Questions (Chicago, IL: University of Chicago Press, 2014).*

DOT I // God

2 *Bronnie Ware, Top 5 Regrets of the Dying (California, USA: Hay House Inc., 2012)*

3 *Ware, Top 5 Regrets of the Dying.*

4 *Harvard Second Generation Study (website), 2015, https://www.adultdevelopmentstudy.org.*

5 *Victor Frankl, Man's Search for Meaning (Boston, MA: Beacon Press, 1959).*

6 *Richard Dawkins, The God Delusion (Boston, MA: Mariner Books, 2008).*

DOT II // YOURSELF

7 *Musonius Rufus, That One Should Disdain Hardships, trans. Cora Lutz (Connecticut, USA: Yale University Press, 2020)*

8 *St. Augustine, On Christian Teaching, trans. R.P.H. Green, 1st ed. (Oxford, UK: Oxford University Press, 2008).*

9 *James Edward Stroud, The Knights Templar & The Protestant Reformation (Florida, USA: Xulon Press, 2011).*

10 *Ryan Holiday, The Obstacle is the Way (New York, NY: Portfolio, 2014).*

11 *Lucius Annaeus Seneca, Moral and Political Essays, ed. J. F. Procopé (New York, NY: Cambridge University Press, 1995).*

12 *Ryan Holiday and Stephen Hanselman, Lives of The Stoics (Westminster, England: Portfolio Press, 2020).*

13 *Frankl, Man's Search for Meaning.*

14 *Epictetus, Discourses and Selected Writings.*

15 *Marcus Aurelius, Meditations (1797), ed. Gregory Hays (New York, NY: Penguin Random House, 2003).*

16 *Zig Ziglar, See You at the Top (New Orleans, LA: Pelican Publishing, 1977).*

17 *Martin Seligman, Learned Optimism (New York, NY: New York Knopf, 1990).*

18 *Seligman, Learned Optimism.*

19 *Seligman, Learned Optimism.*

20 *Bushnell, Sermons for the New Life 21, http://articles.ochristian.com/article11990.shtml*

21 *Tyrtaeus, Fragments, ed. James W. Bailey (Whitefish, Montana: Kessinger Publishers, LLC, 2010). https://www.amazon.com/Martial-Fragments-Tyrtaeus/dp/1290954577/*

22 *William Smith (ed.), The Dictionary of Greek and Roman Biology and Mythology (London, England: Taylor and Walton, 1844).*

23 *Epictetus, Discourses and Selected Writings.*

24 *Aurelius, Meditations.*

25 *Aurelius, Meditations.*

26 *Lucius Annaeus Seneca, Dialogues and Essays, eds. Tobias Reinhardt and John Davie (Oxford, England: Oxford University Press, 2007).*

27 *Keith Craft, "Choose Your Hard." Warrior Night, Elevate Life Church, Frisco, Texas. May 16, 2019.*

28 *Mike Berardino, "Mike Tyson explains one of his most famous quotes," South Florida Sun-Sentinel, November 8, 2012, https://*

www.sun-sentinel.com/sports/fl-xpm-2012-11-09-sfl-mike-tyson-ex-plains-one-of-his-most-famous-quotes-20121109-story.html.

29 Failure Is Not an Option," Wikipedia, December 18, 2020, https://en.wikipedia.org/wiki/Failure_Is_Not_an_Option.

30 Gene Krantz, Failure is Not an Option (New York, NY: Simon & Schuster, 2009).

31 Philostratus the Elder and Philostratus the Younger, Imagines, trans. Arthur Fairbanks (Cambridge, MA: Harvard University Press, 1931).

32 Aulus Gellius, Attic Nights, trans. John C. Rolfe (London, UK: Loeb Classical Library, 1927).

33 Lucius Annaeus Seneca, Letters From a Stoic, trans. Robin Campbell (London, England: Penguin Classics, 1969).

34 "Everybody Cheats?" Chicago Tribune, June 23, 2005, https://www.chicagotribune.com/news/ct-xpm-2005-06-24-0506240277-story.html.

35 Aurelius, Meditations.

36 James Stockdale, Thoughts of a Philosophical Fighter Pilot (California, USA. Hoover Institution Press, 1995).

37 Stockdale, Thoughts of a Philosophical Fighter Pilot.

38 William Ernest Henley, "Invictus" (poem) (United Kingdom: Vanity Fair, 1888).

39 Stockdale, Thoughts of a Philosophical Fighter Pilot.

40 Jim Collins, Good to Great (New York, NY: Harper Collins, 2001).

41 Aurelius, Meditations.

42 Epictetus, Discourses and Selected Writings.

43 Paul Brians et al., Reading About the World Vol 1, 3rd ed. (San Diego, CA: Harcourt Brace, 1999), https://www.amazon.com/Reading-About-World-Vol-1/dp/0155674250.

44 Collins, Good to Great.

45 Aurelius, Meditations.

46 Aurelius, Meditations.

47 Tertullian, Delphi Complete Works of Tertullian (Illustrated) (Sussex, UK: Delphi Ancient Classics, 2018).

48 Heraclitus, Fragments, trans. Brooks Haxton (London, England: Penguin Classics, 2003).

49 Epictetus, Discourses and Selected Writings.

50 Aurelius, Meditations.

51 Friedrich Nietzsche, On The Genealogy of Mortals and Ecce Homo, ed. Walter Kaufman (New York, NY: Vintage, 1989).

52 Ryan Holiday, "An Interview with the Master: Robert Greene on Stoicism," Daily Stoic, accessed May 6, 2022, https://dailystoic.com/robert-greene-interview/.

53 Robert Burns, "To a Mouse," Scottish Poetry Library, 1785.

DOT III // YOUR ROLE

54 Dr. James Allan Francis, "One Solitary Life," Bartelby 916, 1963, 1–7, https://www.bartleby.com/73/916.html.

55 Gregory a. Smith, "About Three-in-Ten U.S. Adults Are Now Religiously Unaffiliated," Pew Research Center, December 14, 2021, https://www.pewresearch.org/religion/2021/12/14/about-three-in-ten-u-s-adults-are-now-religiously-unaffiliated/.

56 William Henry Herndon, Herndon's Lincoln Vol. 3: The True Story of a Great Life, (London, England: Forgotten Books, 2010).

57 Aurelius, Meditations.

58 Brennan Manning, The Ragamuffin Gospel (Sisters, OR: Multnomah Books, 1990).

59 Andy Stanley, "What Love Requires," North Point Community Church, published February 22, 2015, https://northpoint.org/messages/brand-new/what-love-requires.

60 *Jack Stuef, "A Remembrance of Forrest Fenn," Medium. com, published September 23, 2020, https://thefinder.medium. com/a-remembrance-of-forrest-fenn-1be2a8646ff2.*

61 *Ben Westcott, "Is this the world's largest pearl? It's been under a bed for 10 years," CNN Style, August 25, 2016, https://www.cnn. com/style/article/largest-pearl-philippines-amurao/index.html.*

62 *Bill Hull, Conversion and Discipleship (Grand Rapids, Michigan: Zondervan, 2016).*

63 *C. S. Lewis, Mere Christianity, (New York, NY: HarperCollins Publishers, 1952).*

64 *You Are Not a Human Being Having a Spiritual Experience. You Are a Spiritual Being Having a Human Experience," Quote Investigator, June 20, 2019, https://quoteinvestigator.com/2019/06/20/ spiritual/*

65 *Craft, Your Divine Fingerprint.*

66 *Craft, Your Divine Fingerprint.*

67 *Plato, Phaedo (Oxford World's Classics), trans. David Gallop (Oxford, England: Oxford University Press, 2009).*

68 *"You Are Not a Human Being Having a Spiritual Experience."*

69 *Lan, "The Inscribed Unknown Tombstone," Enjoy a Simple Life, published July 15, 2015, https://enjoyasimplelife.blogspot. com/2015/07/the-inscribed-unknown-tombstone.html*

70 *Craft, Your Divine Fingerprint.*

71 *Jake Christian, "Great Quotes: It's My Job to Love," Deeper (blog), August 18, 2011, https://jakechristian.wordpress. com/2011/08/18/great-quotes-its-my-job-to-love/*

72 *Aurelius, Meditations.*

73 *Plutarch, How to Be a Leader: An Ancient Guide to Wise Leadership, trans. Jeffrey Beneker, (Princeton, New Jersey: Princeton University Press, 2019).*

74 *Dr. Martyn Lloyd-Jones, The Christian Warfare: An Exposition on Ephesians 6:10 to 13 (Ada, Michigan: Baker Books, 1998).*